# ESSE **...**

**Naples and the Amalfi Coast:** Regions and Best places to see

 Best places to see 34–55

 Featured sight

Naples 83–114

Bay of Naples 115–138

 The Amalfi Coast 139–153

**Original text by Jack Altman**
Updated by Tim Jepson

© Automobile Association Developments Limited 2007
First published 2007

ISBN-10: 0-7495-4964-5
ISBN-13: 978-0-7495-4964-0

Published by AA Publishing, a trading name of Automobile Association Developments
Limited, whose registered office is Fanum House, Basing View, Basingstoke,
Hampshire RG21 4EA.
Registered number 1878835.

Automobile Association Developments Limited retains the copyright in the original
edition © 2001 and in all subsequent editions, reprints and amendments

A CIP catalogue record for this book is available from the British Library

Colour separation: MRM Graphics Ltd
Printed and bound in Italy by Printer Trento S.r.l.

A02694
Maps in this title produced from mapping © MAIRDUMONT / Falk Verlag 2005

# About this book

**Symbols are used to denote the following categories:**

➕ map reference to maps on cover

✉ address or location

☎ telephone number

🕐 opening times

✋ admission charge

🍴 restaurant or café on premises or nearby

Ⓜ nearest underground train station

🚌 nearest bus/tram route

🚆 nearest overground train station

⛴ nearest ferry stop

✈ nearest airport

❓ other practical information

ℹ tourist information office

► indicates the page where you will find a fuller description

This book is divided into five sections.

**The essence of Naples and the Amalfi Coast** pages 6–19
Introduction; Features; Food and Drink; Short Break including the 10 Essentials

**Planning** pages 20–33
Before You Go; Getting There; Getting Around; Being There

**Best places to see** pages 34–55
The unmissable highlights of any visit to Naples and the Amalfi Coast

**Best things to do** pages 56–79
Good cafés and restaurants; top activities; stunning views; places to take the children and more

**Exploring** pages 80–153
The best places to visit in Naples and the Amalfi Coast, organized by area

**Maps**
All map references are to the maps on the covers. For example, Pompei has the reference ➕ 29R– indicating the grid square in which it is to be found

**Prices**
An indication of the cost of restaurants and cafés at attractions is given by € signs: €€€ denotes higher prices, €€ denotes average prices, € denotes lower prices

**Hotel prices**
Price are per room per night: € budget (under €100); €€ moderate (€100–€125); €€€ expensive to luxury (over €125)

**Restaurant prices**
Price for a three-course meal per person without drinks: € budget (under €15); €€ moderate (€15–€33); €€€ expensive (over €33)

# Contents

# The essence of...

Naples is southern Italy's great city, pulsing with life, full of wonderful buildings and museums and flanked by an idyllic bay. The city is famed as much for its citizens as for its monuments, and there is nowhere else in Italy where you can find such a level of life lived on the streets. The bustle of city life is complemented by the stunning natural beauty of the Amalfi coast with its heady mix of cobalt blue sea, plunging cliffs, and citrus fruit groves. The awesome strength of nature is also evident in the region as visitors to the unique and poignant Pompei will testify.

features

Unlike more businesslike northern cities, Naples evokes the legendary Italian image of warm-hearted exuberance but with an intriguing dark side. Most of Naples' great art is baroque and that goes for the people, too. Baroque art is imbued with a sense of the melodramatic, of movement and a certain tension. This is as true of outraged butchers and triumphant fishmongers along the Via dei Tribunali as it is of exultant angels and tormented saints in the church of San Gregorio Armeno. People stage a street-corner *sceneggiata* (performance) several times a day for some choice insult, parking ticket or other catastrophe. Comparing Neapolitans to their

monuments is easier now that the *centro storico* (historic centre) is getting a much-needed facelift. But rest assured, for every lovingly restored church or *palazzo*, another is still tottering on in a perversely beautiful state of decay. In Naples, this also is life, sometimes more so than a too artificial renovation. Just as sublime, pizza is treated in its birthplace not as vulgar fast food, but as a noble delicacy, and the tomato as a fruit of the gods.

Vesuvius offers the Bay of Naples an enchanting backdrop and an ever-present menace. Pompei, its ancient victim, retains its houses, shops, bakery and brothel. Out in the bay, Capri valiantly protects the charms of its greenery and blue grottoes; while

along the Amalfi Coast, a gracious world apart beckons with Ravello's elegant villas, the medieval monuments of Amalfi town, and clusters of houses clinging to the hillside of Positano.

food & drink

Like the best of Italian food, Neapolitan cuisine is simple, savoury and colourful. The tomato is king, the basis of all dishes *alla napolitana*. Historians question whether Naples invented the pizza but nowhere else is it such a gourmet delicacy. And from the Sorrento peninsula and Amalfi Coast comes the great variety of fresh seafood and exquisite mozzarella.

Portions are generous, but in these more health-conscious times, there is no longer the pressure to eat the whole gamut of *antipasti* (starters), a *primo piatto* (first course) of, say, pasta, then a fish or meat *secondo piatto* (second course), followed by fruit, pastry, coffee and a liqueur. Instead you can have a light starter, pasta and salad, and then an ice-cream at a nearby *gelateria*.

### STARTERS

Many restaurants offer *bruschetta* (toasted Italian bread) with chopped tomatoes, onions and olives. For more substantial *antipasti*, try a seafood salad of *calamari* (squid), *polpi* (octopus) or *alici* (fresh anchovies); the popular *insalata caprese*, Capri's salad of sliced mozzarella, tomatoes and basil; or a *peperonata* of green, red and yellow peppers baked in olive oil,

onions, tomato and garlic. *Minestra maritata* is a hearty soup of pork or chicken with chicory, usually served the day after a big feast.

## PIZZA AND PASTA

The purists' classical Neapolitan pizza is the *margherita*. First created in 1889 at Naples' Brandi pizzeria (➤ 108) for Queen Margherita of Savoy, it bears the colours of the Italian flag: red tomatoes, white mozzarella and green basil. Variations are numerous, with seafood, such as *cozze* (mussels), mushrooms, *salsicce* (sausage), scattered with a layer of cold *rucola* (rocket) or the folded *calzone* (pocket pizza), but always with a characteristically fine crust baked in a wood-fired brick oven.

Naples' favourite pasta dishes use simple sauces

of tomato, garlic and olive oil for *vermicelli alla napolitana*, sometimes spiced up with hot red chilli pepper *(all'arrabbiata)*, or melted ricotta cheese for the little spiral *fusilli*. Best known of the seafood sauces is *alle vongole*, with Venus clams. More spectacular is the black pasta *(linguine al nero)* in a delicious sauce of finely chopped squid cooked in its own ink.

## FISH AND MEAT DISHES

Best of the locally caught fish are *spigola* (sea bass), *spada* (swordfish), *triglie* (red mullet) or *cefalo* (grey mullet), again served grilled or with a tomato and oregano sauce. Two traditional

Neapolitan beef dishes are *bistecca alla pizzaiola* (sliced beef in a tomato, garlic and oregano sauce), and *braciolone napoletano* (a hearty and filling meat loaf).

## DESSERTS

Neapolitan pastries can be a delight: try honeyed *struffoli*, iced chocolate *mustaccioli*, *zeppola* (doughnuts) and sweet ricotta-filled *sfogliatelle*, best with a cappuccino at breakfast.

## WINES AND LIQUEURS

The volcanic soil of the Vesuvius vineyards produces some honourable whites, rosés and reds, bottled under the Vesuvio label, as well as the famous *Lacrime di Cristo* dessert wines, fruity and sparkling. White wines from Ravello, Ischia and Capri all go well with seafood. The most popular liqueur, served ice-cold, is the lemon-flavoured *limoncello*, with Sorrento, Amalfi and Capri all claiming to produce the best. Other locally produced liqueurs are *Mirtillo* (bilberry) and *Finocchietto* (fennel).

**short break**

If you have only a short time to visit Naples and the Amalfi Coast and would like to take home some unforgettable memories the following suggestions will give you a wide range of sights and experiences that won't take very long, won't cost very much and will make your visit very special. If you only have time to choose just one of these, you will have found the true heart of the region.

● **Go to the Teatro San Carlo** for an opera or concert in one of the world's most beautiful theatres. It is tough competing with Neapolitans for tickets to the opera and classical music concerts at the Teatro San Carlo. Usually your only hope at the theatre box office itself is for returns. Otherwise, your best bet is through a major hotel, with an extra commission charge, or through a commercial ticket agency.

If you are unable to get tickets you can take an out-of-season tour of the interior (➤ 105).

● **Order a Pizza Margherita,** the classical choice, at the Pizzeria di Matteo on Via dei Tribunali, the destination of pizza gourmets (➤ 110). Naples is well-known as the home of the pizza. Its history goes back to Greek times when Neopolis was a Greek colony. Although pizzas are now popular all over the world it is believed by many that the best are still found in Naples.

● **Visit the sumptuous Chapel of San Gennaro** in Naples cathedral, where believers see the blood of the martyred saint liquefy every May and September (➤ 92). The liquefaction of San Gennaro's blood happened originally just once a year, on the anniversary of its first occurrence one

miraculous September day. Suddenly – cynics say in response to popular demand – it also began happening on the saint's feast day in May.

● **Sit at the elegant Caffè Gambrinus** (➤ 60), one of the most famous cafés in Naples, with a cappuccino and crispy *sfogliatella* pastry and watch the world go by on Piazza Trieste e Trento.

● **Escape the turmoil of city traffic** in the gracious convent garden tucked away behind the

Church of San Gregorio Armeno (➤ 90–91). Naples has few tranquil public squares because the Church appropriated all the best open spaces. Here you can sit on a stone bench in the shade of the garden's wonderful citrus trees. In the centre is a marble fountain decorated with dolphins, sea-horses and spouting masks, and flanked by statues of Jesus and the Woman of Samaria.

● **Admire Caravaggio's masterpieces** at the Capodimonte Museum (➤ 44–45) and his altar painting in the Pio Monte della Misericordia church (➤ 98). The couple of years that this violent, brilliant, tormented painter spent in Naples at the end of his life left an indelible mark on the city's art.

● **Take a siesta** under the cooling umbrella pines in the gardens of Ravello's Villa Cimbrone (➤ 147)

or Villa Rufolo (➤ 54–55) and then wake up to the stupendous views of the Amalfi Coast.

● **Stand in the Pompei bakery** and look over the ancient ovens at Vesuvius, brooding on the horizon, quiet for the time being (➤ 128). If you are drawn by what you see you can walk up the volcano, which takes about 30 minutes. The edge of the crater provides a very dramatic view inside.

● **Cruise around Capri** in a boat from Marina Grande harbour and explore the island's many grottoes, not just its most celebrated Grotta Azzurra (➤ 38–39). Also from the harbour, a funicular takes you up to Capri town.

● **Stroll along the cliffs above Positano** (➤ 46–47), from where there are amazing views of Positano and the emerald green sea. When things get too hot it will be hard to resist a swim at one of the beaches linking the cliff path.

# Planning

# Before You Go

## WHEN TO GO

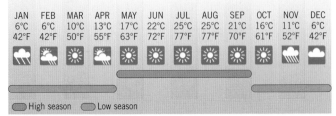

| JAN | FEB | MAR | APR | MAY | JUN | JUL | AUG | SEP | OCT | NOV | DEC |
|-----|-----|-----|-----|-----|-----|-----|-----|-----|-----|-----|-----|
| 6°C | 6°C | 10°C | 13°C | 17°C | 22°C | 25°C | 25°C | 21°C | 16°C | 11°C | 6°C |
| 42°F | 42°F | 50°F | 55°F | 63°F | 72°F | 77°F | 77°F | 70°F | 61°F | 52°F | 42°F |

High season    Low season

Temperatures are the **average daily maximum** for each month.

The best time to visit Naples is from May to September, when the temperature range is pleasant and most areas and attractions are not too busy. Within that period, however, expect disruption and increased crowds over the Easter weekend.

August should be avoided, mostly because of the heat but also because many shops, restaurants, clubs and bars close for part of the month.

In winter you'll find the atmosphere is amazing in December when people descend to buy *presepi* (Christmas crèches), but it is very crowded.

## WHAT YOU NEED

● Required
○ Suggested
▲ Not required

Some countries require a passport to remain valid for a minimum period (usually at least six months) beyond the date of entry – contact their consulate or embassy or your travel agent for details.

| | UK | Germany | USA | Netherlands | Spain |
|---|---|---|---|---|---|
| Passport (or National Identity Card where applicable) | ● | ● | ● | ● | ▲ |
| Visa (regulations can change – check before you travel) | ▲ | ▲ | ▲ | ▲ | ▲ |
| Onward or Return Ticket | ▲ | ▲ | ▲ | ▲ | ▲ |
| Health Inoculations (tetanus and polio) | ▲ | ▲ | ▲ | ▲ | ▲ |
| Health Documentation (► 23, Health Advice) | ● | ● | ▲ | ● | ● |
| Travel Insurance | ○ | ○ | ○ | ○ | ○ |
| Driving Licence (national) | ● | ● | ● | ● | ● |
| Car Insurance Certificate (if own car) | ○ | ○ | ○ | ○ | ○ |
| Car Registration Document (if own car) | ● | ● | ● | ● | ● |

## ADVANCE PLANNING
### WEBSITES
● Naples Tourist Board
**www.**inaples.it
● Italian Tourist Board **www.**enit.it
● Italian Government Tourist Board
**www.**italiantourism.com

### TOURIST OFFICES AT HOME
**In the UK**
Italian State Tourist Board
✉ 1 Princes Street, London W1R
8AY ☎ 020 7408 1254

**In the USA**
Italian Government Travel Office
(ENIT)
✉ 630 Fifth Avenue, Suite 1565,
New York NY 10111
☎ 212/245 4822

Italian Government Travel Office
(ENIT)
✉ 12400 Wilshire Boulevard, Suite
550, Los Angeles, CA 90025
☎ 310/820 1898 or 310/820 9807

## HEALTH ADVICE
**Insurance**
EU nationals receive medical and
hospital treatment with the relevant
documentation – a European Health
Insurance Card (EHIC) for Britons –
and pay a percentage for
medicines. Medical insurance is still
advised. US visitors should check
their insurance coverage.

**Dental services**
Nationals of EU countries can
obtain dental treatment at reduced
cost at dentists which operate
within the Italian health service. A
qualifying document (EHIC for
Britons) is needed. Still, private
medical insurance is advised for all.

**www.**ehic.org.uk

## TIME DIFFERENCES

| GMT | Italy | Germany | USA (NY) | Netherlands | Spain |
| --- | --- | --- | --- | --- | --- |
| 12 noon | 1PM | 1PM | 7AM | 1PM | 1PM |

Naples is one hour ahead of GMT,
six hours ahead of New York and
nine hours ahead of Los Angeles.

Clocks go forward one hour for
summer time.

## WHAT'S ON WHEN

**January** *Costume Parade* (New Year's Day) in the Piazza Umberto I, Capri.
Procession for Children (Epiphany, 6 Jan). Piazza del Plebiscito, Naples.
Costumed nativity play at Stazione Marittima, Naples.
Burning of Christmas Trees (17 Jan), Naples.

**February** Carnival – five days of parades and parties in Capua.
Carnival – masked parades through *centro storico*, Naples.

**April** Easter – re-enactments of the Stations of the Cross; hooded processions of lay fraternities on Sorrento peninsula.
*Pasquetta* (Easter Monday) – many Neapolitans take picnicking excursions out to the country.
Pizza baking contest on Naples' Piazza Mercato.
Liberation Day (25 April) – celebration of World War II invasion by the Allies.

**May** *Labour Day* (1 May).
*Maggio Sacro* (first Sun) – procession from the Duomo to Santa Chiara, Naples. The first of two annual commemorations of the liquefaction of San Gennaro's blood.
International Regatta, Capri (➤ 151).

**June** Open-air concerts – start of the summer season of classical music in the courtyards of Castel Nuovo, Castel Sant'Elmo and Castel dell'Ovo, Naples.
Jazz concerts in Ravello.

**July** The summer music festival commemorates Wagner and other composers' residence at the Villa Rufolo, Ravello (➤ 54–55).
*Madonna del Carmine* is celebrated by fireworks at Piazza Mercato, Naples, simulating the burning of the campanile.
Midnight concerts – start of the

## NATIONAL HOLIDAYS

| JAN | FEB | MAR | APR | MAY | JUN | JUL | AUG | SEP | OCT | NOV | DEC |
|-----|-----|-----|-----|-----|-----|-----|-----|-----|-----|-----|-----|
| 2 | | 1 | (2) | 1 | | 1 | | | | 1 | 3 |

| | |
|---|---|
| **1 Jan** | New Year's Day |
| **6 Jan** | Epiphany *(Befana)* |
| **March/April** | Easter Sunday, Easter Monday |
| **25 April** | Liberation Day |
| **1 May** | Labour Day |
| **15 August** | Assumption *(Ferragosto)* |
| **1 Nov** | All Saints' Day |
| **8 Dec** | Immaculate Conception |
| **25 Dec** | Christmas Day |
| **26 Dec** | Santo Stefano |

Most shops, offices and museums close on these days.

summer arts season featuring music, films and cabaret in the public parks.
*Sant'Anna* (25 Jul) – procession of illuminated boats for the patron saint of Ischia.

**August** *Ferragosto* (15 Aug) – Assumption Day festivities include music and games throughout Naples.

**September** Pizza festival in Naples. *San Gennaro's Feast Day* (19 Sep) – the second commemoration of the liquefaction of the saint's blood in the Duomo, Naples.

**October** Start of the autumn classical music season at the Conservatory and *palazzo* courtyards, Naples.

**November** Opera – opening of Teatro San Carlo's opera season, Naples.

**December** There is a Christmas market on Via San Gregorio Armeno, Naples.
There are general seasonal festivities throughout the *centro storico* in Naples.

# Getting There

### BY AIR
The main entry point for Naples and the Amalfi Coast is Naples' Capodichino Airport (**www**.gesac.it ☎ 081 789 6259). You can catch an 'Alibus' express shuttle bus, which leaves every 30 minutes (6.30am–11.50pm) and takes 20 minutes to get to Piazza Garibaldi. Travelling from Naples back to the airport buses run from 6am to midnight. ☎ 800-639525 (toll free); **www**.anm.it

### BY CAR
Drive on the right.

You may choose to drive through Europe to Naples, which is about 1,750km (1,090 miles) from London. The A1 out of Rome is a good fast route, and there are dual carriageways (divided highways) that bypass the city if you're

heading to the coastal resorts, or the Amalfi Coast.

Speed limits: motorways (autostrade), for which there are tolls, are **130kph (80mph)**; main roads **110kph (68mph)**; secondary roads: **90kph (55mph)**; urban roads: **50kph (30mph)**.

Seat belts must be worn at all times where fitted.

Random breath-testing is carried out; never drive under the influence of alcohol.

Petrol is a little cheaper in Italy than in Britain and many other European countries, and diesel (gasolio) tends

to be cheaper than unleaded *(senza piombo)*. Outside urban areas petrol stations open 7am to 12.30pm and 3 to 7.30pm. Most are closed on Sundays. Credit cards are rarely accepted.

In the event of a breakdown, ☎ 116, giving your registration number and type of car and the nearest ACI (Automobile Club d'Italia, **www.**aci.it) office will assist you. You will be towed to the nearest ACI garage. This service is free to foreign-registered vehicles or cars rented from Rome or Milan airport.

## BY BUS

Long distance buses travel from London to Rome, where you have to change bus to continue on your journey to Naples. It is a long, though rewarding, trip, but you will eventually arrive in Piazza Garibaldi.

## BY TRAIN

Most visitors travelling to Naples by train arrive at Stazione Centrale station in Piazza Garibaldi, the main junction for most other local services. Trains services operate to Naples from all over Italy and it is a very cheap and efficient way to travel.

# Getting Around

## PUBLIC TRANSPORT

### INTERNAL FLIGHTS

Services throughout the country are provided by the national airline Alitalia (☎ **www**.alitalia.it) to Capodichino Airport (☎ 081 789 6259, **www**.gesac.it). The flight time to Naples from Rome is 60 minutes and from Milan 75–85 minutes.

## TRAINS

The national rail network is run by Trenitalia (**www**.trenitalia.it) sometimes referred to by its former name, the Ferrouie dello Stato. The Intercity train reaches Rome from Naples in 2 hours and the Treno Eurostar is 15 minutes faster. Trains provide good service around the Bay of Naples, the Circumvesuviana to Pompei and Sorrento, and the Cumana to Pozzuoli and Baia.

## REGIONAL BUSES

SITA (☎ 081 552 2176; www.sita-on-line.it) provides a good regular service between Naples (Via Pisanelli, near Piazza Municipio) and the Amalfi Coast resorts all the way to Salerno. In the other direction, SEPSA buses (☎ 081 542 9965; www.sepsa.it) leave Piazza Garibaldi for Pozzuoli and Baia.

## BOAT TRIPS

Ferries and the much faster hydrofoils leave from two main piers in Naples' harbours. From Molo Beverello, Caremar (☎ 081 199 123199; www.caremar.it) serves Capri, Ischia and Sorrento. Alilauro (☎ 081 497 2222; www.alilauro.it) serves Ischia from Mergellina. Capri is also linked directly to both Positano and Sorrento.

## URBAN TRANSPORT

A 'Giranapoli' ticket is valid for 90 minutes' travel on city buses, trams, metro, funicular, Ferrovia Cumana and Circumflegrea. A day ticket is also available.

## TAXIS

Taxis are available in all towns and tourist resorts. They can be hailed, though you'll be lucky to find one passing when you want it. Otherwise find a rank (at stations and *piazze*), or call a radio taxi (in Naples ☎ 081 552 5252 or 081 556 4444).

## CAR RENTAL

Car rental is available in most cities and resorts from international and Italian companies, but it is not cheap. Generally local firms offer better rates but cars can only be booked locally. Air or train travellers can get special inclusive deals.

## CONCESSIONS

Most national museums and other sights in and around Naples offer considerable price reductions for children – even free for under-18s at Museo di Capodimonte and Museo Archeologico. Children under 12 travel at reduced fare, often half price, on most trains and ferries, free under 4. For longer trips along the Amalfi Coast, beyond Salerno, to Paestum and back, consider the *Carta Famiglia* family group-ticket, available from main stations. This gives a 30 per cent discount for a family of four travelling together. Restaurants rarely propose menus with reduced prices for children's portions, but usually accommodate specific requests, such as splitting one portion between two. Similar concessions are offered for senior citizens over 65.

# Being There

## TOURIST OFFICES

✉ Piazza del Gesù Nuovo 7 ☎ 081 551 2701 🕔 Mon–Sat 9–1.30 (Apr–Oct also 3.30–7)

✉ Palazzo Reale, Piazza del Plebiscito 1 ☎ 081 252 5720/081 252 5711 🕔 Apr–Oct Mon–Sat 9–1.30, 3.30–7; Nov–Mar Mon–Sat 9–1.30

✉ Via San Carlo 9 ☎ 081 402394 🕔 Apr–Oct Mon–Sat 9–1.30, 3.30–7; Nov–Mar Mon–Sat 9–1.30

Official website for visitor information: **www.inaples.it**

## EMBASSIES AND CONSULATES

**UK** ☎ 081 423 8911
**Germany** ☎ 081 248 8511
**Netherlands** ☎ 081 551 3003
**Spain** ☎ 081 411 157
**USA** ☎ 081 583 6111

## MEDIA

The tourist office provides listings of current and upcoming events, and publishes a monthly magazine for tourists, *Qui Napoli*, in English and Italian. The most up-to-date information for Naples and its surrounding region is in the daily newspaper: either Naples' own *Il Mattino*, or the national *La Repubblica*, which includes a good section for the region's cultural events.

For the Naples area (which includes Capri, Ischia, Pompei, Sorrento and the Campi Flegrei), Naples Tourist Office (✉ Via San Carol 9 ☎ 081 402394) provides a complete official accommodation listing *(Napoli e Provincia: Annuario Alberghi)* detailing amenities and prices for the year of publication. Similar information for the Amalfi

Coast is available through each individual resort's tourist office.

## TELEPHONES

Telephones are in public places and almost every bar. They take 20 or 50 cent or 1 euro coins, and more often credit card or phonecards *(schede telefoniche)*, which you can buy for 5 or 10 euros. Phonecards are available from Telecom Italia offices, tobacconists and stations. All numbers in Naples start with 081; toll-free numbers start with 800.

## OPENING HOURS

- Shops
- Offices
- Banks
- Museums/Monuments
- Churches

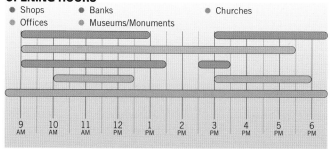

| 9 AM | 10 AM | 11 AM | 12 PM | 1 PM | 2 PM | 3 PM | 4 PM | 5 PM | 6 PM |

General opening hours for shops are: 9 or 10am –1 or 1.30 and 3 or 4–7.30 or 8. Department stores and shops in tourist areas may stay open all day and sometimes later in the evening. Some shops are closed Monday morning, others on Saturday afternoon or all day. Most close on Sunday. Winter opening times may be a little shorter. Banks are closed during lunch (usually 1.20–2.20) and at weekends. Museum times are erratic and should always be checked for changes. Last entries are normally an hour before closing.

### EMERGENCY TELEPHONE NUMBERS

**Police** 112
**Fire** 115
**Ambulance** 113

### INTERNATIONAL DIALLING CODES

**UK** 00 44
**USA/Canada** 00 1
**Irish Republic** 00 353
**Australia** 00 61
**Germany** 00 49
**International operator** 170

### POSTAL SERVICES

The Italian postal system can be slow. Premium-rate 'Posta Prioritaria' is a faster service. In Naples the main post office is at

Piazza Matteotti 2 ☎ 081 552 0502; **www**.poste.it. Larger post offices open 8am to 6.30pm (to 12.30pm Saturday), other offices: 8am to 1.30 or 2pm (to 11.45am Sat). Closed Sun.

## ELECTRICITY

Power supply: 220 volts. Socket: usually round two- hole taking plugs of two round pins. British visitors should bring an adaptor; US visitors will need a voltage transformer.

## CURRENCY

The euro is the legal currency of Italy. Euro notes come in denominations of 5, 10, 20, 50, 100, 200 and 500. Coins are 1, 2, 5 bronze-coloured euro cents and 10, 20 and 50 gold-coloured euro cents. In addition there is a 1 euro coin with a silver centre and gold surround and 2 euro coin with a gold centre and silver surround.

## HEALTH AND SAFETY

**Sun advice** From June onwards, the summer sun can get dangerously hot, particularly in unshaded archaeological sites like Pompei. Use plenty of sunscreen, wear a hat and drink lots of water.

**Drugs** Pharmacies (*farmacia*), recognised by their green cross sign, have highly trained staff who are able to offer medical advice on minor ailments and provide a wide range of prescription and non-prescription medicines and drugs.

**Safe water** It is quite safe to drink tap water and water from drinking fountains, but never drink from a tap marked *acqua non potabile*. However, many Italians prefer the taste of bottled mineral water, which is widely available.

**Personal Safety** The *Carabinieri* (military-style-uniforms and white shoulder belts) deal with general crime and public order. The worst problem (really be on your guard for this) is theft and pickpockets.
● Carry shoulder bags slung across your body.
● Don't wear expensive jewellery or carry large sums of money.

## TIPS/GRATUITIES

| | | |
|---|---|---|
| Yes ✓ | No ✗ | |
| Restaurants (if service not included) | ✓ | 15–20% |
| Cafés/ Fast-food outlets | ✗ | |
| Bars | ✓ | 15–20% |
| Taxis | ✓ | 15–20% |
| Porters | ✓ | €1–€2/bag |
| Chambermaids | ✓ | €1–€2/week |
| Cloakroom attendants | ✓ | €1 |
| Hairdressers | ✓ | €3 |
| Toilets | ✗ | |

- In the city consider carrying your passport and credit cards in a pouch or belt.
- Keep on the inside of the pavement.
- Lock car doors and never keep valuables in your vehicle.

## PHOTOGRAPHY

**Light:** beware of the often dazzling light of southern Italy.

**Where you can photograph:** most museums and certain churches will not allow you to photograph inside; check first.

**Film and developing:** a roll of film is called *pellicola* but 'film' should get you understood. Developing film or digital photographs can be expensive.

## CLOTHING SIZES

| Italy | UK | Rest of Europe | USA | |
|---|---|---|---|---|
| 46 | 36 | 46 | 36 | |
| 48 | 38 | 48 | 38 | |
| 50 | 40 | 50 | 40 | |
| 52 | 42 | 52 | 42 | |
| 54 | 44 | 54 | 44 | **Suits** |
| 56 | 46 | 56 | 46 | |
| 41 | 7 | 41 | 8 | |
| 42 | 7.5 | 42 | 8.5 | |
| 43 | 8.5 | 43 | 9.5 | |
| 44 | 9.5 | 44 | 10.5 | |
| 45 | 10.5 | 45 | 11.5 | **Shoes** |
| 46 | 11 | 46 | 12 | |
| 37 | 14.5 | 37 | 14.5 | |
| 38 | 15 | 38 | 15 | |
| 39/40 | 15.5 | 39/40 | 15.5 | |
| 41 | 16 | 41 | 16 | |
| 42 | 16.5 | 42 | 16.5 | **Shirts** |
| 43 | 17 | 43 | 17 | |
| 36 | 8 | 34 | 6 | |
| 38 | 10 | 36 | 8 | |
| 40 | 12 | 38 | 10 | |
| 42 | 14 | 40 | 12 | |
| 44 | 16 | 42 | 14 | **Dresses** |
| 46 | 18 | 44 | 16 | |
| 38 | 4.5 | 38 | 6 | |
| 38 | 5 | 38 | 6.5 | |
| 39 | 5.5 | 39 | 7 | |
| 39 | 6 | 39 | 7.5 | |
| 40 | 6.5 | 40 | 8 | **Shoes** |
| 41 | 7 | 41 | 8.5 | |

# Best places to see

# 1 Duomo di Amalfi

**Rising above a monumental stairway, the imposing cathedral is the perfect expression of Amalfi's past as a medieval maritime power.**

The oldest part of the largely Romanesque cathedral dates back to the 10th century when Amalfi's ships criss-crossed the Mediterranean to ply their trade with Arab and Persian potentates – and occasionally to plunder the cargoes of rivals from Pisa, Genoa and Venice. The exotic tastes of the eastern Mediterranean are reflected in the Arabian-style interlocking arches and majolica-tiled ornament on the church and its 13th-century campanile set at an angle

to the façade. The bronze Byzantine door was made in Constantinople in 1065 by Simeon of Syria and was presented to the city by Pantaleone Di Mauro, an Amalfitan merchant of legendary wealth.

The porticoed atrium at the top of the stairway, rebuilt along with the façade in the 19th century, connects the older Cappella del Crocifisso (Crucifix Chapel) to the main part of the cathedral. Inside the beautifully restored chapel are fine 15th-century frescoes of the *Enthroned Madonna, Christ in Majesty* and the mystic

*Marriage of St Catherine.* Completed in 1276, the cathedral was expanded to house the relics of St Andrew in its crypt. The reputed remains of the first Apostle were brought here from Constantinople to be buried under the main altar, designed by Domenico Fontana.

To the left of the atrium, the Chiostro del Paradiso (Cloister of Paradise) was built by Archbishop Filippo Augustariccio in 1266 as a cemetery for the Amalfitan aristocracy. Today, the quadrangle is a haven of quiet, the palm trees and slender-columned, pointed arches another reminder of the city's ancient links with the Middle East.

✚ 29Q ✉ Piazza del Duomo, Amalfi ☎ 089 871 059
🕐 Jun–Oct daily 9.30–7; Nov–May 9.30–5.15 (times may vary) ✋ Duomo free; Crypt and Chiostro del Paradiso inexpensive
🍴 Cafés, restaurants (€–€€€)
ℹ Corso Repubbliche Marinare 19 ☎ 089 871 107

# 2 Grotta Azzurra, Capri

**Revered by the ancient Romans, the cave with its ethereal blue light has been counted among the world's most celebrated natural sights.**

The Blue Grotto is not just a tourist attraction to be dismissed because of its huge popularity; the mysterious natural light is truly magical. Only special flat rowing boats can get through the mouth of the cave, a mere 2m (6ft) wide and with barely 1m (3ft) headroom. The cavern interior is 54m (117ft) long, 15m (50ft) high and 30m (100ft) wide. The grotto owes the unique luminosity of its waters and play of light on the walls to sunlight refracted through the grotto's original opening which subsided below sea level several centuries ago.

In the Galleria dei Pilastri (Gallery of Columns) it is possible to see traces of an ancient Roman landing stage and caverns with stalactites. Around AD 30, Emperor Tiberius built his Villa Damecuta at this end of the island and constructed the quay and a nymphaeum (shrine to the water nymphs) in the cave – marble statues of marine deities discovered here in 1964 are now exhibited at Certosa di San Giacomo. The smaller Villa Gradola, directly above the cave, was linked to the landing stage by underground passages.

German poet Augustus Kopisch and Swiss painter Ernst Fries rediscovered the cave in 1826 when cruising around with a local fisherman.

Delirious with joy, they swam in and out of the cave
and then rushed to Naples to spread the news.
Almost overnight, the Grotta Azzurra established
Capri's reputation as an island of romance.

✚ 27Q ✉ Capri 🚹 Marina Grande ☎ 081 837 0634
🕔 Daily 9 to one hour before sunset ✋ Expensive
🍴 None 🚌 From Anacapri 🚣 Motor or rowing boat from
Marina Grande

# 3 Monte Vesuvio

**www.**parconazionaledelvesuvio.it

**This beautiful menace, overlooking the Bay of Naples, last erupted in 1944 and continues to exert its magnetism on both villagers and visitors.**

The earliest picture of Vesuvius is from a house in ancient Pompei showing a pretty mountain covered in woods and vineyards. That fresco, now in Naples' Museo Archeologico (➤ 42–43), was buried in the famous eruption of AD79. Today, 700,000 people live on the slopes, some in houses only a few hundred metres from the crater. More than 2,000 years after it first exploded into life, it

looks peaceful enough – no white plume from the summit and, even up close, just a few steaming fumaroles. But Vesuvius is just sleeping, not dead. After the Pompei catastrophe, seven major eruptions occurred before 1032 and several minor ones up to the 14th century. The volcano then lay dormant for over 300 years. In 1631, it exploded again, splitting its southern flank and burying 4,000 villagers in molten lava, ash and boiling mud. In recent centuries, the most spectacular eruption came in 1872 when a new cone opened on the north flank. Major 20th-century eruptions occurred in 1906, decapitating the cone and spouting a fountain of gas and lava 600m into the air, and eerily during an Allied bombing raid in 1944.

The volcano today has two peaks, the original Somma (1,132m/3,714ft) and the newer Vesuvio (1,277m/4,190ft), with a crater 600m (1,970ft) wide and 200m (655ft) deep. The road from Ercolano winds through woodland and sombre lava fields to a car park, with a 20-minute walk to the crater. On the way, the **Museo dell'Osservatorio Vesuviano** has audiovisual displays of volcanic activity.

➕ 28S ✉ Parco Nazionale del Vesuvio 🕓 Access to crater from sunrise to one hour before sunset ✋ Climb to crater moderate 🍴 Café/restaurant (€) at summit car park
🚍 Transporti Vesuviani ☎ 081 559 3173 bus from Piazzale Stazione Circumvesuviana, Ercolano 🚉 Ercolano (Circumvesuviano line from Naples)
ℹ Via IV Novembre 82–84 Ercolano ☎ 081 788 1243
**Museo dell'Osservatorio Vesuviano**
☎ 081 610 8483; www.ov.ingv.it 🕓 Daily 10–2 (by appointment only)

# 4 Museo Archeologico di Napoli

**Proximity to the great Roman sites of southern Italy has enabled Naples to create one of the best endowed archaeological museums in Europe.**

Ideally, any projected visit to Pompei and Herculaneum should begin here. In the relative tranquillity of the museum at the top of busy Via Santa Maria Costantinopoli, you can get a sense both of the immense riches of sculpture, painting and mosaics recovered from the buried cities and of comparable treasures brought here from Rome. Like the Capodimonte Museum (► 44–45), the Archaeological Museum was originally founded in 1777 to house the private collections of the Farnese family. To these were added findings from the Roman cities buried by Vesuvius, along with other collections from ancient Greece and Egypt.

The best way to tackle the collection is to start on the first floor, with paintings from Pompei and Herculaneum, and work your way down. First-floor highlights include the famous dual portraits of Paquius Proculus and his wife, a splendid Hercules watching his child Telephus being suckled by a doe, and artwork from Pompei's Temple of Isis. There is also a fine 19th-century detailed scale model of the excavated city of Pompei. On the mezzanine floor are the great mosaics of Alexander the Great defeating Darius of Persia, and exquisite bird and animal scenes. Perhaps most famous of all are the erotic paintings, mosaics and sculpture kept in the adults-only Gabinetto Segreto (Secret Cabinet).

The ground floor's most important pieces are the Roman marble statues from the Farnese collection. *The Tyrannicides*, *Hercules* and *Dirce and the Wild Bull* are invaluable copies of long-lost masterpieces from classical Greece (5th–4th century BC).

✚ 8B ✉ Piazza Museo Nazionale 19, Napoli ☎ 081 544 1494 🕑 Mon, Wed–Sun 9–8. Last entry 6pm. Closed 1 Jan, 1 May, 25 Dec ✋ Expensive, Gabinetto Segreto extra 🍴 Cafés, restaurants (€–€€) 🚇 Piazza Cavour 🚌 24, 47, 110 ❓ Audio tours and lectures. The Gabinetto Segreto can only be visited by guided tour, advance booking required

# 5 Museo di Capodimonte

**In a hilltop park overlooking the city, the Bourbons' 18th-century palace houses one of Italy's most important art museums.**

The Museo di Capodimonte brings art and nature together to provide a soothing escape from the city hustle. After decades of neglect, the collections of predominantly Italian Renaissance and baroque paintings hang once more in the handsomely renovated rooms of the elegant Bourbon palace. The park's landscaped gardens are a bonus: lawns among groves of pine, holm oak, maple and cedar, fragrant eucalyptus and magnolia, and a grand view over the city and Bay of Naples. King Charles of Bourbon (Carlo di Borbone) chose the site in 1739 as hunting grounds and added a porcelain factory

(still here). In the palace he hung the art collections of his mother, Elisabetta Farnese, for which the museum was created in 1957.

On the first floor, the Farnese Gallery (rooms 2–30) houses several masterpieces of Italian and Flemish art from the 15th–17th centuries. Highlights include Masaccio's *Crucifixion* (1426), Mantegna's portrait of the 16-year-old Cardinal Gonzaga (1461), Titian's sensual *Danae* (1545, hidden from public view in more prudish times), Parmigianino's exquisite *Antea* (1535, now an emblem of Capodimonte), and Pieter Brueghel's

*Parable of the Blind* (1568). On the same floor (rooms 31–60) are the palace's royal apartments showing fine porcelain and objects of decorative art from the Borgia family collection. The second floor exhibits Neapolitan art with pieces from the city's churches. These include Simone Martini's lovely *St Ludovic of Toulouse* (1317, from San Lorenzo Maggiore, ➤ 100) and Caravaggio's *Flagellation of Christ* (1609, from San Domenico Maggiore). A third floor displays modern art.

➕ 8F ✉ Via di Miano 1, Napoli ☎ 081 749 9111 (recorded information) or 081 749 9109 🕐 Thu–Tue 8.30–7.30. Park daily 8 to one hour before sunset. Closed 1 Jan, Easter Sun, 1 May, 15 Aug, 25 Dec 👆 Expensive; park grounds free 🍴 Ground floor café (€) 🚌 24, 110, R4

# Positano

**This elegant resort pours its dazzling white houses and pretty little gardens over the hillside like a cornucopia.**

Positano is popularly believed to have been settled by refugees from Paestum (► 142–143) – Greek Poseidonia – hence its name. Certainly it shares today with those ancient Greek colonists an undeniable taste for good living. The only monument of note is the originally Romanesque **Church of Santa Maria Assunta** with a large majolica-tiled dome added in the 18th century. On the high altar is a 13th-century Byzantine-style Black Madonna, and medieval bas-relief carving on the campanile. Positano is a delightful place in which just to hang out, eat the seafood, shop on Via dei Mulini in the fashionable boutiques and to use as a base for sightseeing.

There are plenty of pleasant walks, short and long. From the popular Spiaggia Grande beach, take the cliff walk west past an old Spanish watchtower to the less crowded Spiaggia Fornillo. On the hillside above this beach, climb up to the belvedere for a great view over Positano. Other swimming coves – Ciumicello, Arienzo, La Porta – may be accessible

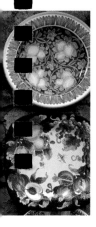

only by boat. The caves here were some of the coast's earliest dwellings, La Porta's having revealed artefacts from the Stone Age. A little further afield, directly overlooking Positano, take the bus up to Montepertuso and walk back down.

✚ 29Q ❚❚ First-class cafés, restaurants (€–€€€) on Marina Grande 🚌 SITA between Sorrento and Salerno 🛥 Amalfi Coast (TravelMar ☎ 089 871 483/089 875 959)
ℹ️ Via del Saracino 4 ☎ 089 875 067

**Church of Santa Maria Assunta**
✉️ Via Marina ☎ 089 875 480 🕐 Daily 8.30–12.30, 3.30–5.30. Closed during services

7

# Spaccanapoli, Naples Old Town

**The thoroughfare that splits the historic centre of Naples traces the great moments of the city's story – medieval, Renaissance and baroque.**

Viewed from the hill of Certosa di San Martino (► 89), Spaccanapoli slices through the Naples of mansions, churches and university buildings, each with concealed gardens and cloisters, to the Forcella district of craftsmen's workshops. What was once a main artery of ancient Greek Neapolis today changes its name along the way from Via

Benedetto Croce to Via San Biagio dei Librai, intersected by side streets preserving the grid plan of antiquity. Piazza del Gesù is the entrance to the Graeco–Roman city, where the Jesuits transformed a 15th-century palace into their Church of Gesù Nuovo (➤ 95). Near by is the fortress-like Church of Santa Chiara and its exquisite cloister-garden (➤ 100–101).

Palazzo Venezia (No. 19) was the home of the Venetian ambassadors. Via Benedetto Croce opens out onto Piazza San Domenico with its charming café, pastry shop, the Gothic Church of San Domenico Maggiore (➤ 98–99) and the elegant russet Renaissance façade of the Palazzo Corigliano. Via San Biagio dei Librai is dedicated to the patron saint of booksellers, who had their shops here. The 15th-century Palazzo Carafa Santangeli has a marble portal with Roman statues above its wooden doors. Inside the 16th-century charitable bank of Monte di Pietà is a chapel with a ceiling fresco (1618) by Belisario Corenzio.

✚ 9A ⊠ Via Benedetto Croce, Via San Biagio dei Librai ⊗ Most churches and several *palazzi* open daily 9–2 🍴 Good cafés, restaurants and pizzerias (€–€€) 🚌 In the pedestrian zone ❓ There are informative signposts for principal monuments on the itinerary of the tourist office's *museo aperto* (open museum)

# 8 Tempio di Nettuno, Paestum

**www.**infopaestum.it

**Best preserved of the ancient monuments in the Greek city of Paestum, this 2,500-year-old temple is a marvel of Doric power and simplicity.**

Paestum was originally named Poseidonia and this temple was popularly thought to be dedicated to the city's protective deity, the sea-god Poseidon – known as Neptune to the Romans. Scholars now believe it is more likely to have been the temple of Hera or Zeus. It appears to have been modelled on the Greek motherland's Temple of Zeus at Olympia. Colonists from the city of Sybaris (on the south Italian coast's Gulf of Taranto) built it around 460BC, perhaps 30 years after settling in Paestum.

The excellent state of preservation of this masterpiece of the classical era gives a complete idea of what most Greek temples were like. Solidly planted on its platform, the temple has retained its architrave, entablature, frieze of metopes and triglyphs, and a pediment supported by a Doric peristyle of six columns on the front and 14 columns along the sides. It measures 20m (66ft) by 60m (197ft). In the interior, a *pronaos* (vestibule) precedes a vast *cella* (central chamber), with the nave separated from its two side aisles by rows of double columns. Placed at the front of the temple are altars for the ritual sacrifice of animals, and for the placing of fruit and other offerings.

The popularity of Paestum on the Grand Tour undertaken by British and American gentlemen in the 18th and 19th centuries was such that elements from sketches of the Temple of Neptune showed up on the façades of banks, museums and plantation mansions from London to Louisville.

🕀 32P ✉ Via Magna Grecia, Paestum ☎ 082 881 1023
🕐 Daily 9 to one hour before sunset; Museum: daily 9–7 (closed 1st and 3rd Mon of the month) 🎟 Site moderate; site and museum expensive 🍴 Café (€) 🚌 From Salerno (Piazza della Concordia) 🚆 Paestum (from Salerno)
ℹ Via Magna Grecia 887 ☎ 082 881 1016

# Villa dei Misteri, Pompei

**www.**pompeiisites.org

**One of the finest of Pompei's villas, the Villa dei Misteri is famous for its cycle of frescoes of life-size figures enacting the rituals of the Dionysiac cult.**

The Villa of the Mysteries stands outside the Porta Ercolano, the ancient city gate to Herculaneum, at the end of Via dei Sepolcri, a street lined with the monumental tombs of prominent Pompeian citizens. The villa was a grand country house, the residence of a prosperous gentleman farmer and wine-grower. It was probably built in the 2nd century BC, renovated around 60BC and then again just before the eruption of Vesuvius in AD79. It was built on ground sloping down to the sea, then much closer than it is today, with terraces and porticoes offering fine views. Frescoes show the patrician family's taste for the good life in the fashionable Hellenistic manner.

Through the east entrance, visitors reached the villa's spacious peristyle or colonnaded courtyard. Kitchens are off to the south and the *torcularium* (room for wine production) lies to the north. Two massive wooden winepresses (one reconstructed with a carved ram's head)

crushed out the last juices of the trampled grapes into terracotta jars set in the floor.

Residential quarters are grouped around an atrium west of the peristyle. The bedrooms *(cubicula)* are enhanced by *trompe l'oeil* frescoes of elegant arched porticoes opening out to gardens and other buildings. An open living room *(tablinum)* has delicately detailed frescoes of Egyptian deities painted on a dramatic black background. The dining room *(triclinium)* is decorated on three sides with the magnificent fresco-cycle that gives the villa its name: ten richly coloured scenes of a young bride's initiation into the Dionysiac mysteries – a sensual cult much appreciated in the wine-growing region of Campania.

🕀 29R ✉ Via dei Sepolcri, Pompei Scavi ☎ Zona Archeologica 081 857 5347 🕓 Apr–Oct daily 8.30–7.30, Nov–Mar 8.30–3.30. Closed 1 Jan, Easter Mon, 15 Aug, 25 Dec 💷 Expensive, ticket includes main site and Villa dei Misteri. Joint ticket available, for entry to five sites, including Herculaneum ❓ English-language tours 🍴 Cafeteria (€) 🚊 Pompei– Scavi (Villa dei Misteri) ℹ Via Sacra 1 ☎ 081 850 8451

# 10 Villa Rufolo, Ravello

**With their view of the Amalfi Coast, the gardens of this exquisite 13th-century villa inspired both writer Boccaccio and composer Wagner.**

Opposite the Duomo on Piazza del Vescovado, a medieval square tower stands at the entrance to one of the most enchanting villas in all southern Italy. The buildings, dating back to the 13th and 14th centuries, rise on hillside terraces overlooking the sea. Arabic influence is apparent in the ornate architecture, especially in the intertwining pointed arches of the cloister-like courtyard. The villa's chapel has an interesting antiquarium of ancient Roman and medieval sarcophagi, funeral urns and architectural fragments.

With their umbrella pines and majestic cypresses, the gardens are heavy with the fragrance of exotic plants. From the terrace, look down over the domes of Ravello's little 13th-century Annunziata church to the coastal village of Atrani. The villa has attracted popes and kings, and it was in these gardens that Giovanni Boccaccio walked with his beloved Fiammetta when escaping from his office job in Naples in 1330. He devoted one of his famous stories in *The Decameron* to the villa's wealthy owner, Landolfo Rufolo, who resorted to piracy to break the competition of merchants from Genoa.

Over 500 years later, German composer Richard Wagner took the Villa Rufolo's gardens as his model for the Garden of Klingsor in his last opera, *Parsifal*, a solemn religious drama begun here in 1877 and produced at Bayreuth in 1882. Ravello celebrates this inspiration every summer with an open-air festival of Wagner's and other composers' music performed in the Rufolo gardens.

✠ 29R ✉ Piazza del Vescovado, Ravello ☎ 089 857 657 ⚅ Daily 9 to sunset ✋ Moderate 🍴 Café/restaurant (€–€€) 🚌 SITA bus once daily from Naples, hourly from Amalfi 6am–9pm ❓ Festival Musicale di Ravello ☎ 089 858 149; www.ravelloarts.org ℹ Piazza del Duomo 10 ☎ 089 857 096

# Best things to do

# Ways to be a local

**Take your cappuccino** in the morning standing up at a bar. Neapolitans take their breakfast *(prima colazione)* standing at the counter, a cappuccino or a kick-start *ristretto*, a thimbleful of concentrated espresso, and a crisp *sfogliatella* or softer *cornetto* (croissant) with jam or sweet ricotta filling.

**Call out 'Bravo!'** at the Teatro San Carlo, for the tenor; 'Brava!' for the soprano. Apart from making you feel part of the local scene it's great fun.

**Order a pizza** in a gourmet restaurant. Neapolitans still pride themselves on producing the best pizzas in the world.

**Buy a Totocalcio lottery ticket** at a street kiosk. Doing the lottery is a favourite pastime for many Neopolitans, and you may even win.

**Join in the *passeggiata*** on romantic Piazza di San Domenico. This quintessentially Italian ritual sees the streets full with locals, out to see and be seen while meeting up with friends.

**Read *Gazzetta dello Sport*** on the terrace of the Caffè Gambrinus along with the many others who make this their first port of call before starting a busy day. Be sure to sample the famous espresso or cappuccino while your're here.

**Rent a Vespa** motor-scooter to get around the Sorrento peninsula. This is a great way to explore the coastline and take in the spectacular views; but take care and don't attempt to drive as the locals do.

**Sip a *Pantera Rosa* (Pink Panther) cocktail** at the Gran Caffè on Capri's Piazzetta. This is Capri's main haunt for locals in the evening after the day-trippers have left. Put your glad rags on as you could be rubbing shoulders with the rich and famous.

**Waggle the flat of your hand**, palm down, to signal that something is 'not bad, could be better'. Watch and observe and you will see the experts at work before attempting it yourself.

# Good cafés and restaurants

### LA CAFFETTIERA

Sit indoors in the tea room or on the fashionable terrace outside from where you can watch the smart people of the Chiaia quarter. Neopolitan pastries are served here, including the delicious *baba* cakes and crispy *sfogliatelle* pastry.

✉ Piazza dei Martiri 25, Naples ☎ 081 764 4243.

### GAMBRINUS

A venerable and elegant tea room and an enjoyable place for people-watching. Dating from 1860, this is Naples oldest café and something of an institution.

✉ Piazza Trieste e Trento, Naples ☎ 081 417 582.

### GRAN CAFFÈ

Join the charming islanders for an apéritif on the terrace after your meal and fully appreciate this beatiful island.

✉ Piazzetta Umberto I, Capri ☎ 081 837 0388.

### INTRA MOENIA

A funky café/bookshop that is great favourite with students and writers. The calming atmosphere provides a good bolt hole from the hectic street life outside

✉ Piazza Bellini 70, Naples ☎ 081 290 720.

### O PARRUCCHIANO

Nicknamed La Favorita, this Sorrento institution does a roaring trade all year round. The recommended dishes here are cannelloni, gnocchi and fish simply grilled with a little lemon.

✉ Corso Italia 71 ☎ 081 878 1321

### POLLIO

Come here for Sorrento's best pastries; it attracts big crowds in high season.

✉ Corso Italia 172, Sorrento ☎ 081 878 2190.

### LA SAVARDINA DA EDOARDO

There is a lovely walk from Capri Town to this charming trattoria in a citrus garden. Try linguine in herbs, cherry tomatoes, garlic and fresh anchovy or raviloi with *caciotta* cheese.

✉ Via Lo Capo
☎ 081 837 6300

### SCATURCHIO

Delicious pastries right on one of the city's most handsome squares. The *sfogliatelle* is superb.

✉ Piazza di San Domenico 19, Naples ☎ 081 551 6944.

### VILLA BRUNELLA

Sample some the best cuisine Capri has to offer at this hotel's terrace restaurant with a romantic vista of Marina Piccola.

✉ Via Tragara 24, Capri
☎ 081 837 0122.

### LA ZAGARA

Try the famous chocolate cake while you sit in the shade of the lemon trees.

✉ Via dei Mulini 6/8, Positano ☎ 089 875 964.

# Top activities

### CANOEING

Hire a boat or canoe from Bagni Le Sirene Marina Piccola on Capri
and explore the amazing grottoes that surround the island.
✉ Via Mulo 63, Capri ☎ 081 837 0221.

### DIVING

With its rich aquatic wildlife and submerged Greek and Roman
sites, the Bay of Naples and the Amalfi Coast are wonderful places
to go diving; Sea Point Italy offer diving classes geared to all
different levels supervized by a team of qualified instructors.
✉ Via Molo di Baia 14, Baia ☎ 081 868 8868; www.seapointitaly.it

### FISHING

The Amalfi Coast is a better spot for fishing than the Bay of
Naples. No licence is required for sea fishing from shore or boat.

### FOOTBALL

As far as religion goes, football comes just after, and for many
just before, the Catholic church. In his heyday, taxis carried effigies
of (now-disgraced) Argentine star Maradonna next to the

Madonna. You can see the Naples team, Napoli, play in the two-tiered San Paolo stadium.

✉ Piazzale Vincenzo Tecchio, Naples ☎ www.calcionapoli.it ❓ Tickets: Via Francesco Galeota 19 (☎ 081 593 40001; www.napolisoccer.it)

## HOT SPRINGS
Pay a visit to Ischia's Nuove Terme Comunale (public spa facilities) to indulge in thermal treatments, mudbaths and massage.
✉ Via delle Terme, Ischia ☎ 081 984 376.

## MOUNTAIN-BIKING
Many of the Amalfi Coast's resorts hire bicycles for you to explore the back country.

## MOUNTAINEERING
One of the most exhilarating experiences is climbing Vesuvius or the Lattari mountains behind Amalfi. If you fancy a trekking or climbing excursion visit the website of the local Club Alpino Italiano branch.
✉ Via Trinita degli Spagnoli 41, Naples ☎ www.cainapoli.it

## SAILING
The best sailing is from Posíllipo harbours in Naples, or Positano, Amalfi, Capri and Ischia. The Bay of Naples' major sporting event is Capri's international regatta held in May. Regional regattas may be held in summer at the major Amalfi Coast resorts – and Naples, too. For details, check with the tourist information offices at Positano, Amalfi and Naples.

## WALKING
Self-guided or accompanied walking tours on the Amalfi Coast and the Sorrento peninsula are organized by ATG-Oxford.
✉ 69–71 Banbury Road, Oxford ☎ 01865 315678 (brochure line 01865 315665)

# from Piazza Dante to Forcella

**Walk by way of Piazza Bellini from Via dei Tribunali's aristocratic *palazzi*, churches and markets to the workshops of Forcella. Visit the treasures of San Gregorio Armeno (➤ 90–91), San Lorenzo Maggiore (➤ 100), the Duomo (➤ 92) and Pio Monte della Misericordia (➤ 98).**

*After a quick peek at the narrow streets of the Quartieri Spagnoli (Spanish Quarter) west of the Via Toledo off Piazza Dante, take the arched gateway left off the piazza to cut through Via Port'Alba to Piazza Bellini.*

Luigi Vanvitelli designed Piazza Dante's monumental crescent in 1757 – now embracing a 19th-century statue of Dante. Students throng the bookshops in the Via Port'Alba arcade and the café terraces of Piazza Bellini, overlooking remains of the ancient Greek city walls (4th century BC).

*From the southeast corner of Piazza Bellini, take Via San Pietro a Maiella and cross Piazza Miraglia to continue along Via dei Tribunali, with short digressions to churches right on Via San Gregorio Armeno, left on Via Duomo.*

San Pietro a Maiella convent houses the Conservatorio di Musica. Via dei Tribunali is the central of three ancient *decumanus* streets, crossing the Greek agora and Roman forum on Piazza San Gaetano. Fruit, vegetable, fish and meat markets like those in today's arcades have been here for 2,500 years.

*Back on Via dei Tribunali, turn right at the church of Santa Maria della Pace on Via della Pace. Cross Via Vicaria Vecchia to enter Via Forcella forking to the right across Piazza Calenda to Corso Umberto I.*

The names of the side streets here testify to the time-honoured crafts of bustling Forcella: *intagliatori* (wood-carvers), *candelari* (chandlers), *armaioli* (gunsmiths) and *chiavettieri* (locksmiths).

**Distance** 2km (1.2 miles)
**Time** 2–3 hours, with visits to churches and street markets
**Start point** Piazza Dante ✚ 8A 🚌 R1, R4
**End point** Forcella ✚ 10A 🚌 R2 on Corso Umberto I
**Lunch** Pizzeria di Matteo, a monument in itself (€)
✉ Via Tribunali dei 94 ☎ 081 455 262

# Stunning views

Naples and the harbour from Capodimonte (➤ 44–45).

Spaccanapoli from Certosa di San Martino (➤ 89).

Bay of Naples from Vesuvius (➤ 40–41).

Vesuvius from Santa Lucia (➤ 102).

Capri's Faraglioni rocks from Parco Augusto (➤ 117).

Island of Capri from Sorrento cliffs (➤ 132).

Pompei's amphitheatre from the top seats, facing Vesuvius (➤ 130).

Along the Amalfi Coast from Vietri near Salerno (➤ 145).

Amalfi from the gardens of Ravello's Villa Rufolo (➤ 54–55).

# Places to take the children

### BEACHES

Ischia's north coast offers the best sandy beaches for family
swimming and water sports. A popular beach for tourists and locals
on the south coast is the Spiaggia Grande. Positano (➤ 46–47) has
several beaches and coves, fairly close to the harbour. La Porta
has the added attraction of Stone Age cave dwellings to explore.
To reach Capri's best beaches, you have to take a boat.

### BOAT CRUISES

The whole family can enjoy exploring the grottoes on boat cruises
around Capri and along the rugged Amalfi Coast, particularly the
Grotta Azzurra (➤ 38–39) and Grotta di Smeralda (➤ 141).

### MUSEO DI CAPODIMONTE

Even if you cannot coax them inside the museum (➤ 44–45),
children enjoy the pretty palace gardens, so take a picnic – and a
football which, despite signposts to the contrary, is a favourite
pastime there.

### CHRISTMAS FIGURINES

The Neapolitan art of modelling miniature figures for *presepi*
(Christmas mangers) began 600 years ago, inspired by Francis of

Assisi's live re-enactment of the scene at Greccio in 1223. The tradition thrives all year round in workshops around Via San Gregorio Armeno. Children will love to see them at work at Certosa di San Martino (➤ 89), although the most famous workshop is Ferrigno (✉ Via San Gregorio Armeno 8 ☎ 081 552 3148).

## EATING OUT

How can you go wrong in a place that makes the best pizza in the world? In the same restaurant that serves something more sophisticated to their parents kids can have their favourite *quattro stagione*, or discover a pocket *calzone* (actually 'trousers') pizza they can eat with both fists. And then there's the ice-cream!

## EDENLANDIA

This huge funfair is out at Mostra d'Oltremare trade fairgrounds to the west of Mergellina.

✉ Viale Kennedy 76 ☎ 081 239 4090; www.edenlandia.it 🚇 Ferrovia Cumana (Montesanto) to Edenlandia or ANM buses C2, C3 or 152

## OSPEDALE DELLE BAMBOLE

This tiny dolls' hospital in the heart of Spaccanapoli is one of the city's most enchanting shops, and children are captivated by it.

✉ Via San Biagio dei Librai 81 ☎ 081 203 067

## MONTE VESUVIO

Visiting Vesuvius (Monte Vesuvio, ➤ 40–41), and trekking the last stretch to the crater, is quite an adventure for older children.

## POMPEI

Try not to overdo it when taking children to the region's best archaeological sites: Pompei (➤ 128–131) is fine for a couple of hours, but take a good break for lunch. Concentrate on the houses and shops rather than the monuments, though it's fun to test the amphitheatre for its acoustics.

# Naples churches

### CHIESA DI SAN GREGORIO ARMENO

Richly decorated, the church has a fascinating history and boasts beautiful works of art, tranquil cloisters, two organs, and a patron saint who works miracles (➤ 90–91).

### GESÙ NUOVO

This rather grim grey ashlar façade conceals a wealth of baroque riches, Neapolitan art and memories of a modern saint (➤ 95).

### SAN DOMENICO MAGGIORE

A large church standing in one of the busiest piazzas in Naples, with many beautiful works of art (➤ 98–99).

### SAN GIACOMO DEGLI SPAGNOLI

Built in 1540, this fascinating small church reflects the Spanish occupation of the city, and contains the 16th-century tombs of Spanish nobles. To the rear of the altar is the elaborate marble tomb of Don Pedro de Toledo, who built the church.

✉ Piazza Municipio ☎ 081 552 3759 🕓 Tue–Sat 7.30–11, Sun 11–2 🚌 C22, C25, E5, R2, R3

### SAN GIOVANNI A CARBONARA

Intended to house the tombs of the Angevin rulers in the 15th century, this 14th-century chapel is one of the most historically important in Naples. Entry is via a steep flight of steps and inside you will find some magnificent monuments. Most notable is the one high above the altar of King Ladislas. Under the altar is a doorway to the lovely round chapel.

✉ Via San Giovanni a Carbonara 5 ☎ 081 295 873 🕓 Mon–Sat 9.30–1 🚌 181, C68, C83

### SAN LORENZO MAGGIORE

An impressive Gothic church with interesting monuments and a fascinating excavation site underneath (➤ 100).

### SAN PAOLO MAGGIORE

On the site of a Roman temple; pillars can still be seen on the church façade. An impressive staircase leads to the entrance. The huge interior has been restored, and there are some lovely frescoes, and paintings by Stazione and Solimena.
✉ Piazza San Gaetano ☎ 081 454 048 🕓 Mon–Sat 9–12 🚊 E1, R2

### SANTA CHIARA

Rising from the ashes of war, this beautiful church and its enchanting cloisters emanate peace and simplicity (➤ 100–101).

### SANTA MARIA DEL CARMINE

With the tallest campanile in the city it is impossible to overlook this church (➤ 103).

### SANTA MARIA DELLA SANITÀ

Built in 1613, this spacious church is in the pattern of a Greek cross; in the centre is a large dome supported by 24 columns. But the real interest of this formal church lies beneath in the catacombs, where there are traces of frescoes dating back to the fifth century and some gruesome remains from the 17th century, when the skulls were set into the wall – visits are by guided tour.
✉ Via Sanità 124 ☎ 081 544 124 🕓 Mon–Sat 8.30– 12.30, Sun 8.30–1.30 🚊 47, 182, C51, C52, C64, C83

# Pompei ruins

### AMPHITHEATRE
Built in the second century BC – one of the oldest of its kind in existence – the theatre held 5,000 people.
✉ Via Nocera

### FORUM
The oldest part of Pompei, dating from at least the second century. Standing at the highest point, the forum was the heart of political and commercial life.
✉ Via del Foro

### HOUSE OF JULIA FELIX
Home of a wealthy Pompei resident, this large house was rented out as homes and shops, and contained public baths.
✉ Via dell'Abbondanza

### HOUSE OF THE CITARISTA
Two houses once stood here that surrounded many courtyards. The name comes from a statue of Apollo playing a lyre, now in the Museo Archeologico in Naples.
✉ Via Stabiana

## HOUSE OF THE FAUN

The wealth bestowed on this important private residence is apparent in the beautiful wall paintings and the mosaic tiles.

✉ Via della Fortuna

## HOUSE OF THE GOLDEN CUPIDS

The bedroom is the main attraction here with its amazing gold cupids, after which the house is named. Although modest in size, the house has some interesting wall paintings and a restored garden with a pool and sculptures.

✉ Vicolo dei Vetti

## HOUSE OF THE MYSTERIES

Here you will find the best-preserved frescoes in Pompei, which tell the story of a young bride being initiated into the cult of Dionysus. The house was built as an urban villa, but was converted into a country residence around 60BC.

✉ Via dei Sepolcri

## HOUSE OF THE VETII

Owned by wealthy merchants, the house has many well-preserved murals and a lovely garden. The most popular attraction, however, is the room that features famous erotic paintings.

✉ Vicolo dei Vetii

## VIA DELL'ABBONDANZA

As you walk down this street lined with shops, inns and private houses, you can easily imagine people going about their daily life. At the end of the road is the public baths and a brothel.

## VIA DEI SEPOLCRI

This solemn road is lined with tombs carrying inscriptions of the main families of the city; a Roman custom considered a sign of respect. Look for the wheel tracks still indented into the road.

# Piazzas and streets

### PIAZZA BELLINI, NAPLES
Always thronged with people, this lively piazza is the most fashionable spot in the city. Cafés and restaurants and some interesting buildings surround a statue of the composer Vincenzo Bellini looking down on excavations of the old city walls.

### PIAZZA DANTE, NAPLES
Redesigned in the 18th century to accommodate the palace of King Charles III, this large, elegant piazza retains its stately aura. The centrepiece is a statue of Dante.

### PIAZZA DEL PLEBISCITO, NAPLES
The neo-classical harmony of this airy piazza, enclosed in a gracefully curving colonnade, was originally planned in 1810 in secular style. At the centre of the colonnade is the domed Chiesa di San Francesco di Paola. The piazza's two equestrian statues are of Ferdinand and Charles III of Bourbon.

### PIAZZA DEL DUOMO, AMALFI
Amalfi offers, on Piazza del Duomo, a delightfully relaxed atmosphere on the terraces of cafés, ice-cream parlours and restaurants looking across to the cathedral's noble stairway.

### PIAZZA UMBERTO I, CAPRI
The island's capital has at its centre one of the Mediterranean's most fashionable meeting places, Piazza Umberto I, better known as the Piazzetta, more courtyard than square. Its cafés look across to a sturdy clock tower and the quaint Moorish-baroque Santo Stefano church.

### SPACCANAPOLI, NAPLES
The heart of Naples, this historic road encapsulates a wealth of art and architecture, shops, restaurants and bars (► 48–49).

### VIA ANTICAGLIAI, NAPLES

This Roman road is interesting to explore for the remains of its origins. Note the arches across the road which used to link the bathhouse with the playhouse where Emperor Nero performed.

### VIA SCARLATTI

Located in the smart area of Vomero hill, this pedestrianized street upholds the image with its classy shops and plane trees that line both sides. Take a break at one of the tempting cake and ice-cream options during a fun afternoon of retail therapy.

### VIA TOLEDO

Glance above the shop fronts and you will see the facades of many historic *palazzi* in this mostly pedestrianized shopping street on the edge of the Quartieri Spagnoli. When built in the 16th century, it was one of Europe's most elegant streets.

# Great ice-cream

### ALBERTO
Perfect for the island's best loved ice-cream, especially chocolate, and particularly famous for its birthday cakes.

✉ Via Roma 9/II, Capri ☎ 081 837 0622

### ANDREA PANSA
A difficult place to resist, Andrea Pansa has been providing amazing ice-creams and totally delicious white chocolate profiteroles for years.

✉ Piazza Duomo 40, Amalfi ☎ 089 871 065

### BILANCIONE
There are usually long seafront queues for the city's most popular ice-cream parlour. The hazelnut *(nocciola)* has won a Golden Cone *(Cona d'Oro)* in the world ice-cream championships. The exquisite fresh fruit flavours change with the seasons.

✉ Via Posillipo 238/6, Naples ☎ 081 769 1923

### CHALET CIRO
For over 50 years Chalet Ciro has been producing a delicious range of ices and cakes.

✉ Via Caracciolo at Via Orazio, Naples ☎ 081 669 928

## DAVIDE

Unashamedly calls itself *Il Gelato* (The Ice-cream). An astonishing choice of 60 flavours – try the excellent green apple *(mela verde)*.

✉ Via Padre Reginaldo Giuiani 39, Sorrento ☎ 081 807 2092

## FANTASIA GELATI

Exotic combinations of ice-cream are sold here and at the other branches on Via Toledo and Via Cilea.

✉ Piazza Vanvitelli 22, Naples ☎ 081 578 8383

## OTRANTO

For the creamiest concoctions in 30 ever-changing flavours near Certosa di San Martino.

✉ Via Scarlatti 78, Naples ☎ 081 558 7498

## LA SCIMMIA

A pioneer on Naples' gelati scene (it's existed for over 60 years), La Scimmia made its name with classic banana, but it  also does great *crema torrone* (nougat) and pistachio.

✉ Piazza Carità 4 (off Via Toledo), Naples ☎ 081 552 0272

## REMY GELO

Choose from over 30 flavours of ice-cream, as well as many types of granita and frozen yoghurts, plus ice-cream pastries.

✉ Via Ferdinando Galiani 29, Naples ☎ 081 667 304

## LA ZAGARA

Superb ice-cream and pastries in a charming lemon grove; the main attraction is *granita* (iced drinks) of strawberry, lemon, almond and even fig.

✉ Via dei Mulini 6/8, Positano ☎ 089 875 964

# Naples museums and galleries

### CENTRO MUSEI DELLE SCIENZE NATURALI

It's worth seeking out these museums of anthropolgy, mineralogy and zoology. Specimens from all over the world are displayed in a superb hall. Guided tours available.

✉ Via Mezzocannone 8 ☎ 081 253 5163 🕐 Daily 9–1, Mon and Wed 3–5 ✋ Inexpensive. Entry for one museum €1.50, two €2.50, three €3 and all four museums €3.50 🚌 24, E1, R2

### CERTOSA DI SAN MARTINO

This glorious building with superb views and containing a wonderful collection of art is a highlight of a visit to Naples (▶ 89).

### CITTÀ DELLA SCIENZA

This new, well-laid-out science museum has explanations in English as well as Italian. The planetarium and hands-on exhibits will keep children entertained.

✉ Via Coroglio 104 ☎ 081 735 2202; www.cittadellascienza.it ⏱ Tue–Sat 9–5, Sun 10–7; closed Aug ✋ Moderate 🍴 Café 🚌 C9, C10

### MUSEO ARCHEOLOGICO DI NAPOLI

A well organized museum packed with priceless objects that will give you a good insight into the ruins of Pompei (➤ 42–43).

### MUSEO ARTISTICO INDUSTRIALE

Founded in 1878 to display young artists' workmanship, the museum had beautiful pieces of porcelain on show in the museum, some dating back to the 16th century. Note the remarkable flooring from the church of Santa Caterina a Formiello.

✉ Piazzetta Demetrio Salazar 6 ☎ 081 764 7471; www.maimuseum.com ⏱ Mon–Fri 9–1.30 (by appointment only) ✋ Inexpensive 🚌 C25, E5, R3

### MUSEO DI CAPODIMONTE

Appreciate some of the best Italian art and panoramic views at this beautiful palace set on a hill (➤ 44–45).

### MUSEO VILLA PIGNATELLI

A noble neo-classical Doric-columned villa, built in 1826, with beautiful gardens. The villa is home to the Banco di Napoli art collection, while the Museo delle Carrozze (carriage museum) is housed in a separate building and due to reopen in 2007.

✚ 24A2 ✉ Riviera di Chiaia 200 ☎ 081 410 7066/761 2356 ⏱ Wed–Mon 9–2 (last ticket 1pm). Closed Tue ✋ Inexpensive 🚌 R3

### PALAZZO REALE

The seat of power in Naples for three centuries, this elaborate royal palace held one of the most important courts in Europe (➤ 96–97).

# Exploring

This amazing coastline, dominated by southern Italy's main city, Naples, is once again taking the central place in visitors' affection and admiration that it occupied on the Grand Tour of Europe in the 18th and 19th centuries. Then visitors came for the baroque churches and Renaissance palaces, for the grand opera and theatre. They came, too, for the colourful street life and for the good food. All this is still here, with the added spice of joyous modern chaos, for the patient and the curious. The Capodimonte and Archaeological museums have retained a grandeur that makes them a match for any museum in Europe. The monuments are looking better than ever. But nobody comes here expecting to find an immaculate, polished, orderly existence. Naples is a place of real, sensuous life and the people, in their markets and backstreet workshops, have lost none of their natural effervescence.

# Naples

**The city's *centro storico* (historic centre) keeps to the limits of the old Graeco–Roman town, much of it now a pedestrian zone. Almost all the major monuments are located in the narrow triangle formed by the Museo Archeologico, the Duomo (Cathedral) and Piazza del Plebiscito. It is all level going except for the hilltop Certosa di San Martino to the west and the Museo di Capodimonte to the north.**

To tour the city in easy stages, it is a good idea to keep to three or four separate itineraries. Some like to start with an overall view of the city, from the terrace of the Certosa di San Martino or Castel Sant'Elmo. Others like to begin in the thick of it, with Spaccanapoli, which, with leisurely stops at the major sights, can occupy one or two full days, depending on the thoroughness of your visits.

Similarly, it is possible to spend one or two days exploring the Via Tribunali, taking the circular walk beginning at Piazza Dante. Reserve half a day each for an unhurried tour of both the Museo di Capodimonte and Museo Archeologico.

A stroll down Via Toledo (also known as Via Roma) and around Via Chiaia will provide a mixture of sightseeing and shopping, taking in both the fashionable boutiques and the Palazzo Reale and Castel Nuovo. Spare time, too, for the bourgeois Vomero area around the gardens of Villa Floridiana and the celebrated Santa Lucia district down by the harbour.

## CAPPELLA SANSEVERO

The mystery and beauty of its interior make this chapel one of the city's most attractive and intriguing baroque buildings. It is now a museum situated just behind Piazza San Domenico Maggiore (➤ 98–99). Built in 1590 as the Sangro family's private chapel, it became a mausoleum for the princes of Sansevero (Severo was a canonized 4th-century bishop of Naples). In the 18th century, the chapel was given its luminous artistic unity by Don Raimundo de'Sangro, leading figure of the Neapolitan Enlightenment, soldier, scientist, man of letters, Grand Master of the city's Freemasons and brilliant patron of the arts.

The Sansevero ceiling has a joyously coloured fresco, *Gloria del Paradiso* (1749) by Francesco Maria Russo, but the outstanding feature is the chapel's sculpture. Left and right of the arch leading to the high altar are Antonio Corradini's sensual *Pudicizia Veluta* (Veiled Modesty, a homage to Don Raimundo's mother) and Francesco Queirolo's *Disinganno* (Disillusion), an artistic *tour de force* of a man entangled in a net carved entirely in marble. The high altar has a magnificent Deposizione sculpted by Francesco Celebrano. At the centre of the chapel, transferred from the crypt, is Giuseppe Sanmartino's extraordinary *Cristo Velato* (Shrouded Body of Christ).

In addition to the chapel's mystic symbolism, male and female skeletons displayed in a lower chamber, complete with meticulously reconstructed arteries and organs, have provoked speculation about Don Raimundo dabbling in alchemy or black magic. A simpler explanation would be his scientific studies of anatomy and his status as a prominent Freemason.

✚ 8A ✉ Via Francesco de Sanctis 19 ☎ 081 551 8470

⏰ Mon, Wed–Sat 10–6; Sun and
public hols 10–1.30 🚹 Moderate
🍴 Excellent café, pizzeria, restaurant
(€–€€), Via dei Tribunali 🚌 R1

## CAPODIMONTE, MUSEO DI

See pages 44–45.

## CASTEL NUOVO

The formidable seafront fortress
is still known to Neapolitans as
the Maschio Angioino (Anjou
kings' castle keep), though only
a chapel remains from the
13th-century castle. The present
structure was built by Catalan
architect Guillem Sagrera for
Alfonso of Aragon two centuries
later. Its entrance, a white two-
tiered triumphal arch, is a
Renaissance masterpiece by
Pietro de Martino and Francesco
Laurana. The frieze over the
lower arch celebrates Alfonso's
triumphant entry into Naples in
1443. Beneath the pediment's
river gods, and topped by St
Michael, the statues over the
upper arch represent the Four
Virtues (Goodness, Thought,
Knowledge and Wisdom).

A staircase in the inner
courtyard leads to Sagrera's

splendid rib-vaulted Sala dei Baroni (Baronial Hall). The city council now meets where barons were once arrested – many killed on the spot – for conspiring against Alfonso's illegitimate son Ferrante. A Renaissance portal and a rose window have been added to the Anjou kings' Gothic Cappella Palatina (Palace Chapel). Restoration revealed, in the window embrasures, precious fragments of frescoes (1330) by Maso Bianco and his Florentine master, Giotto.

They now form part of the castle's Museo Civico (Civic Museum), along with sculpture by Laurana and Domenico Gagini, and Neapolitan frescoes and paintings from the 15th to 18th centuries.

🚇 20K ✉ Piazza Municipio ☎ 081 420 1241/1342 🕐 Mon–Sat 9–7. Closed 1 Jan, 1 May, 25 Dec 👆 Expensive 🍴 Caffè Gambrinus (€€), good restaurants near by (€–€€) 🚌 24

## CASTEL SANT'ELMO

The massive hilltop citadel, in the form of a six-pointed star, was built by the Spanish in 1537 with tufa stone extracted from its moat. For centuries it was a prison for heretics, revolutionaries and leaders of the Risorgimento movement for Italian unity. The ramparts have a fine view of the city and Bay of Naples.

🚇 17L ✉ Largo San Martino 1, Via Tito Angelini ☎ 081 578 4030 or 081 578 4120 🕐 Thu–Tue 8.30–7.30 (times and prices may vary according to exhibitions). Closed 1 Jan, Good Fri, 1 May, 25 Dec 👆 Inexpensive 🍴 Cafés, restaurants (€–€€) around Vomero's Piazza Vanvitelli 🚡 Funicolare (cable-car) Montesanto

## CERTOSA DI SAN MARTINO

The majestic Certosa di San Martino (Charterhouse of St Martin) is impressive both for its artistic masterpieces and for the grand terrace views of Naples and the harbour. Consecrated in 1368, the richly endowed monastery was expropriated 500 years later by the new Italian state, but preserved as a museum to present its treasures as a representative history of Neapolitan art. Expanding the original conception of Siena's Tino di Camaino, better known as a sculptor, 17th-century architect Cosimo Fanzago gave it its predominantly baroque appearance.

An atrium to the church, on the left of the main courtyard, has frescoes by Belisario Corenzio and Domenico Gargiulo of *Henry VIII's Persecution of English Carthusian Monks*. Striking a more triumphant note for the church's Gothic-vaulted nave, Giovanni Lanfranco's ceiling fresco depicts Christ's Ascension. Of the many chapels don't miss the Cappella di San Gennaro (first left), with paintings by Battistello Caracciolo and sculptures of the Evangelists by Antonio Vaccario. José Ribera's superb *Apostles' Communion* is in the presbytery, and his *Deposition* is on the high altar. See, too, the beautiful 16th-century inlaid walnut panelled wardrobes in the sacristy.

Worth a visit is the Quarto del Priore (Prior's Apartments), with a spiral staircase leading down to a garden. The Chiostro Grande (Great Cloister) has a handsome marble fountain in its charming four-square Renaissance arcaded garden. In the monastery kitchens is a popular display of 18th- and 19th-century *presepi* (Christmas mangers), crowded with lovingly carved shepherds, peasants, angels and animals surrounding the Holy Family.

✚ 17L ✉ Largo San Martino 8 ☎ 081 558 5942 🕐 Thu–Tue 8.30–7.30 (times and prices vary according to exhibitions). Closed 1 Jan, Good Fri, 1 May, 25 Dec 💰 Expensive 🍽 Cafés, restaurants (€–€€) around Vomero's Piazza Vanvitelli 🚋 Funicolare (cable-car) Montesanto ❓ Look for artists at work on figures for *presepi* (Christmas mangers)

## CHIESA DI SAN GREGORIO ARMENO

With its distinctive belfry straddling the narrow Via San Gregorio Armeno, this opulent baroque church is part of a well-endowed convent dedicated to the saint who first took Christianity to Armenia. In 726, nuns fled here with his relics from the Byzantine iconoclastic turmoil in Constantinople. Originally an Eastern Orthodox edifice, the church was rebuilt in the 16th century to meet the demands of the Catholic Counter Reformation, notably with a unified nave and four lateral chapels. Flemish artists created the sumptuous coffered wooden ceiling, with its gilded panels and 16 paintings of martyred saints. In the cupola and on the western wall, Luca Giordano's frescoes (sadly damaged by the humidity) depict St Gregory's martyrdom and the transfer of his relics to Naples. Also in a chapel here, since 1864, are the much-venerated relics of St Patrizia, another refugee from Constantinople.

To the north of the belfry, the convent entrance is at the top of a long stairway. The convent's cloister garden is still beautifully kept, fragrant and shady with orange, lemon and mandarin trees. In the middle, Matteo Bottigliero's monumental marble fountain (1733) has exquisite statues of Christ's meeting with the Samaritan woman. In the convent rooms you'll find many opulent artworks, brought in by novice nuns from wealthy families.

The street outside forms the unofficial centre of Naples' thriving manufacture of traditional figurines for *presepi* (Christmas mangers). The workshops sell their carefully crafted wares – miniature shepherds, sheep, dogs, angels, butchers, bakers and pizza-chefs – all year round, but Via San Gregorio Armeno reaches a bustling crescendo during the Christmas market. *Presepi* can be seen in their most extravagant form at the museum of Certosa di San Martino (➤ 89).

🔼 9A ✉ Via San Gregorio Armeno 44 ☎ 081 552 0186 🕐 Hours vary 🎫 Free 🍴 Cafés, restaurants (€–€€) Via dei Tribunali 🚇 Metro Piazza Cavour

## DUOMO

Steeped in the city's long architectural and spiritual history, the Duomo remains the focus of Naples' celebrated miracle, the annual liquefaction of the blood of its patron saint, San Gennaro. The cathedral stands on a site that has been sacred since the Greeks built a temple here to Apollo. Today's neo-Gothic façade (1905) attempts to recapture the medieval character of the Anjou kings' church, itself incorporating two 4th- and 5th-century Christian basilicas. Evidence of these older structures includes the temple's antique marble columns, the basilica's mosaics and frescoes, and the rib-vaulted chapels of the Angevin-Gothic church, along with the baroque art that followed.

The cathedral has kept its three original Gothic portals, with Tino di Camaino's 14th-century *Madonna and Child* sculpture over the main entrance. Inside, beneath the ornate 17th-century coffered ceiling, the lofty nave has columns taken from ancient Graeco–Roman buildings. In the left aisle, the 4th-century basilica of Santa Restituta has been transformed into a baroque chapel. To the right of the apse the baptistery has graphic mosaic fragments in its dome. Off the right transept is the 13th-century Cappella Minutolo, with mosaic paving, elegant groin vaulting and a monumental tomb with a gabled canopy over the altar.

Most spectacular of all is the Cappella del Tesoro di San Gennaro, a dazzling baroque chapel that attracts the faithful each May and September to see the saint's blood liquefy in phials kept behind the main altar, along with Gennaro's head. Others are content to admire the frescoes of Domenichino and Giovanni Lanfranco and Ribera's painting of San Gennaro emerging unscathed from a furnace.

✚ 10B ✉ Via Duomo 147 ☎ 081 449 097 🕐 Mon–Sat 8–12.30, 4.30–7, Sun 8.30–1, 5–7.30. Closed during services 🖐 Free 🍴 Cafés, restaurants (€–€€) Via Duomo, Via dei Tribunali 🚇 Metro Piazza Cavour 🚌 R2

## GALLERIA UMBERTO I

Among the many quarrels between Naples and Milan is that over who has the finest monumental glass-and-steel shopping gallery? Milan's Galleria Vittorio Emanuele was inaugurated first, in 1878, but Naples' grand neo-Renaissance Galleria Umberto I, built nine years later, may claim to be the more imposing architectural achievement. Replacing the whole neighbourhood of Santa Brigida, ravaged by the cholera epidemic of 1884, it was conceived by architect Antonio Curri as an affirmation of the new Italian state's modern spirit. It was a natural complement to the prestigious Teatro San Carlo (▶ 104–105) and Palazzo Reale (▶ 96–97). The soaring glass-and-steel dome is 57m (187ft) high, above a central mosaic paving of the Zodiac, from which

colonnades branch out, richly decorated with all the polychrome marble and allegorical Graeco–Roman sculptures a prosperous and rather ostentatious 19th-century bourgeoisie could wish for.

In the heyday of Naples' *belle époque*, this precursor of the modern shopping mall attracted high society to the city's smartest cafés, intimate theatres and fashion emporia. Today, the atmosphere is more subdued, but reputable jewellers and other traditional shops remain. Respectable citizens still gather here at that blessed early evening hour of the *passeggiata*, when Italians traditionally take a stroll to discuss the vital issues of the day – forthcoming marriages, football, politics, football, religion and football.

✚ 19K ✉ Main entrance on Via San Carlo ⊛ Arcade open permanently, shops 9–1, 4–7 or 9 or 10–7.30. Closed Sun ✋ Free 🍴 Cafés (€) 🚌 R2

## GESÙ NUOVO

At the west end of Spaccanapoli (▶ 48–49), on a piazza originally just outside the Graeco–Roman city walls, the Jesuits' main church is housed in the 15th-century palace of the Sanseverino princes. (An earlier church, the Gesù Vecchio, stands in the university grounds on Corso Umberto I.) Also on the square, the Guglia dell'Immacolata (Column of the Virgin Mary) replaced, in 1747, an equestrian statue of Spain's Philip V, destroyed by the people, who then had to pay for the Jesuits' lavishly ornate rococo obelisk. The church has kept the Renaissance palace's sober diamond-point embossed façade, adding only the three windows and baroque ornament to the main entrance. The exuberantly colourful interior makes a dramatic contrast. Notice, on the entrance wall, Francesco Solimena's biblical fresco of *Heliodorus Driven from the Temple* and in the left transept Cosimo Fanzago's statues of David and a despondent Jeremiah.

✚ 19M ✉ Piazza del Gesù Nuovo 2 ☎ 081 551 9613 ⊛ Daily 6.45–1, 4–7.30 ✋ Free 🍴 Cafés, restaurants (€–€€) 🚌 R1

## MONTEOLIVETO

Thanks to close ties between Naples' Aragonese court and the Medici and Este princes, Florentine and north Italian art treasures make this 15th-century church a true museum of Renaissance art. In the Cappella Piccolomini (first on the left), Antonio Rossellino designed the monumental tomb for Maria of Aragon and sculpted the altar's splendid nativity bas-relief (1475). In the Cappella Tolosa are glazed terracottas of the Evangelisti by the Della Robbia workshop. Benedetto da Maiano's charming marble relief of the Annunciazione (1489) is in the Curiale chapel. In the Sagrestia Vecchia (Old Sacristy), with its ceiling frescoes by Giorgio Vasari, is Guido Mazzoni's poignant terracotta statue of the Dead Christ.

✠ 19L ✉ Piazza Monteoliveto 44 ☎ 081 551 3333
🕓 Mon–Fri 9.30–12 ♿ Free 🍴 Cafés, restaurants
(€–€€), Via Toledo, Spaccanapoli 🚌 R1
❓ Museum temporarily closed for restoration, telephone before visiting

## MUSEO ARCHEOLOGICO DI NAPOLI

See pages 42–43.

## PALAZZO REALE

What began as a palace for the Spanish monarchy came ultimately, with later additions and transformations, to symbolize the new kingdom of a united Italy. The vast palace complex has five façades, the main one being its entrance on Piazza del Plebiscito. Incorporating the Spanish viceroy's Palazzo Vecchio, Domenico

Fontana designed the Palazzo Reale in a hurry, in 1600, to receive a royal visit from Philip III of Spain, who then failed to turn up. Subsequently, it was the residence of Spanish and Austrian Habsburg viceroys, then the Bourbon and Italian Savoyard kings.

In the 18th century, Luigi Vanvitelli filled in alternate arches of the main façade's arcade with niches. A century later, Umberto I commissioned eight statues of the rulers of the kingdom to illustrate the course of Naples' history from the beginning to its annexation to a united Italy. They underline the fascinating variety of the rulers' origins: Roger of Normandy, Friedrich von Hohenstaufen, Charles d'Anjou, Alfonso I of Aragon, Charles V of Habsburg, Charles Bourbon, Joachim Murat of Napoleonic France and Vittorio Emanuele II of Savoy.

The interior's monumental marble staircase was given its present neo-classical appearance after a fire in 1837. Today's furnishings for the royal apartments , by no means all originals, reflect the style and tastes of the 17th to the 19th centuries. Two charming survivals of the 17th century are the Teatrino di Corte (Court Theatre) and Cappella Reale dedicata all'Assunta (Royal Assumption Chapel).

🚊 19J 🖂 Piazza del Plebiscito 1 ☎ 081 580 8111 🕓 Mon–Tue, Thu–Sun 9–8 (ticket office closed one hour earlier). Closed Wed, 1 Jan, Good Fri, 1 May, 25 Dec ✋ Moderate 🍴 Caffè Gambrinus (€€), restaurants Via Toledo (€–€€) 🚌 R2, R3

## PIO MONTE DELLA MISERICORDIA

A supreme masterpiece of Italian painting rewards a visit to the church of the charitable institution, Monte delle Misericordia, still active after 400 years. On the octagonal church's high altar, Caravaggio's *Opere di Misericordia* (*Works of Charity*, 1606) is one of the most important religious pictures of the 17th century. The Lombard painter uses his mastery of light and shade to illustrate seven acts of charity in one brilliantly grouped composite scene.

The characters come straight from the streets of Spaccanapoli: a grave-digger shrouding a corpse; an irritable girl giving her breast milk to an old man in prison; a tired pilgrim; a gentleman clothing a naked beggar; and even the angels accompanying the Madonna and Child look like Neapolitan street urchins.

Take a look, too, at the seven other altars, each devoted to one of the works of charity, the last (from the right) has a remarkable *Liberazione di San Pietro dal Carcere* (*Liberating St Peter from Prison*) by Battistello Caracciolo, a leading disciple of Caravaggio.

✚ 10B ✉ Via dei Tribunali 253 ☎ 081 446 944/973
🄯 Church and Picture Gallery: Thu–Tue 9–2.30. Closed Wed
🍴 Near by (€–€€) Ⓜ Metro Piazza Cavour 🚌 R2

## SAN DOMENICO MAGGIORE

With its café terraces, elegant palazzi and ornate baroque obelisk, the Piazza di San Domenico is one of the most attractive meeting places in the *centro storico*. Entered through the 16th-century marble portal in its fortress-like apse, the church of San Domenico Maggiore (1283) underwent extensive neo-Gothic restoration in the 19th century. Frescoes (1309) attributed to Pietro Cavallini were recently rediscovered in the Cappella Brancaccio (third right). Left of the nave, the Cappella dei Carafa has a clever *trompe-l'oeil* ceiling fresco of cherubs looking down at a 16th-century *presepe* (Christmas manger). A mausoleum

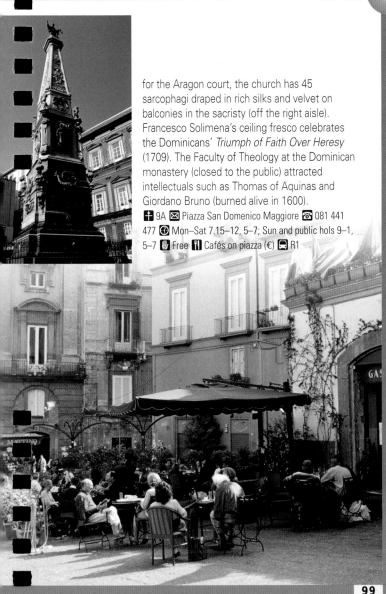

for the Aragon court, the church has 45 sarcophagi draped in rich silks and velvet on balconies in the sacristy (off the right aisle). Francesco Solimena's ceiling fresco celebrates the Dominicans' *Triumph of Faith Over Heresy* (1709). The Faculty of Theology at the Dominican monastery (closed to the public) attracted intellectuals such as Thomas of Aquinas and Giordano Bruno (burned alive in 1600).

✝ 9A ✉ Piazza San Domenico Maggiore ☎ 081 441 477 🕐 Mon–Sat 7.15–12, 5–7; Sun and public hols 9–1, 5–7 👋 Free 🍴 Cafés on piazza (€) 🚌 R1

## SAN LORENZO MAGGIORE

Behind an 18th-century façade is one of southern Italy's outstanding Gothic churches, built in 1266 for Naples' first Franciscan monks by Charles of Anjou. San Lorenzo Maggiore combines French Gothic pointed arches, clustered piers and rib vaulting in the apse and ambulatory with Italian Gothic in the nave's broad walls and truss-beamed ceiling. Among the ambulatory's monumental tombs, notice Tino di Camaino's exquisite shrine for Caterina d'Austria (1323). Neapolitan Giovanno da Nola sculpted the superb high altar (1530) portraying saints Lorenzo, Anthony and Francis of Assisi.

**Excavations** in the courtyard have revealed the Graeco–Roman food market and treasury which once occupied the site.

✚ 9B ✉ Via dei Tribunali 316 ☎ 081 454 948 ⏰ Mon–Sat 7.45am–7pm, Sun 7.45–1, 5.30–7 ✋ Free 🍴 Cafés near by (€–€€) 🚇 Metro Piazza Cavour

**Excavations**
⏰ Mon–Sat 9.30–5.30; Sun 9:30–1.30 ✋ Inexpensive

## SANTA CHIARA AND CHIOSTRO DELLE CLARISSE

The 14th-century church of the Franciscan order of Clarissan nuns, also known because of their oath of poverty as the Poor Clares, is especially beloved for possessing one of the most enchanting cloisters in Italy. With its blind arcades and lofty buttresses, the church itself is quite austere, the façade of yellow tufa stone unadorned except for a rose window above a porch of three pointed arches. Begun in 1328, the free-standing campanile had two upper storeys added in the 16th century. Bombing in 1943 destroyed the church's rich baroque decoration, which had been added in the 18th century, and

reconstruction restored the original, more sober Gothic style. Among the artworks that survived are monumental tombs by Tino di Camaino for Anjou Duke Charles of Calabria and his wife Marie de Valois, on the right wall of the presbytery. Most imposing of all, is the huge tomb of Robert of Anjou (1345) for which Florentine sculptors Giovanni and Pacio Bertini showed the king enthroned and also lying on his deathbed wearing a Franciscan habit.

Entered from outside, behind the church, the Chiostro delle Clarisse, an archaeological area and small museum offer a moment of tranquillity. In 1742, the architect Domenico Antonio Vaccaro divided the cloister garden into four with intersecting vine-shaded alleys. The low majolica-tiled walls and benches show charming scenes of the everyday life of 18th-century citizens. Octagonal pillars are decorated with intertwining vines and wisteria.

✚ 20M ✉ Via Benedetto Croce, Via Santa Chiara 49/c ☎ 081 797 1256
🕐 Church: daily 7–12.30, 4.30–7.30/8.30. Cloister and museum: Mon–Sat 9.30–5.30 (6.30 Apr–Oct), Sun 9.30–1.30 (2.30 Apr–Oct) ✋ Moderate
🍴 Near by (€–€€) 🚌 R1 ❓ Guided and audio tours; occasional lectures and concerts

## SANTA LUCIA

Thanks to the romantic songs of the fishermen and picturesque prints of its waterfront, Santa Lucia was once one of the most popular neighbourhoods in the city. The sailors' church of Santa Lucia a Mare is now set back from the sea since the harbour disappeared under landfill and new construction. The 20th-century promenade formed by Via Nazario Sauro and Via Partenope is lined with luxury hotels, restaurants and yacht clubs, along with a monumental 17th-century fountain, L'Immacolatella, attributed to Pietro Bernini.

On an island joined by a causeway to the Santa Lucia mainland is the Castel dell'Ovo (Castle of the Egg), a former military prison now used for temporary exhibitions. Claimed to be named after the Latin poet Virgil's magic egg, the name is more likely to be due to the castle's shape back in the 14th century.

🚇 19H ✉ Via Nazario Sauro, Via Partenope
🍴 Pizzerias and seafood restaurants (€–€€€)
🚌 R3

## SANTA MARIA DEL CARMINE

The church belongs to a 12th-century Carmelite convent, and has been much changed over the years. The campanile, at 75m (210ft) the city's tallest, acquired its octagonal drum and majolica-tiled spire after a fire in the 17th century, commemorated by spectacular fireworks on the Carmelite feast on 16 July. The original Gothic design is submerged by the extravagant baroque and rococo décor of the 18th century. Neapolitans revere the 14th-century Byzantine icon of the *Madonna Bruna* (*Brown Madonna*) behind the altar and, from the same era, a miraculous wooden Crucifixion in a tabernacle suspended from the ceiling. During a military siege of 1439, the Christ figure is believed to have ducked its head to avoid a shell, thus losing only its crown of thorns.

➕ 23M  ✉ Piazza del Carmine 2  ☎ 081 201 196 or 081 201 942
🕐 Mon–Sat 7–12/12.30 (depending on mass), 5–7.30, Sun and public hols 7–1.30  ✋ Free  🍴 Cafés, restaurants (€–€€) Piazza del Mercato  🚍 R3

## SPACCANAPOLI

See pages 48–49.

## TEATRO SAN CARLO

In 1737, Charles Bourbon commissioned this opera house, dedicated to his patron saint, to rival those of Venice and Rome. It was part of an ambitious building programme that included the Museo Archeologico (➤ 42–43) and the palaces of Capodimonte (➤ 44–45) and Caserta. Coming at a time when Naples was the third largest city in Europe (after London and Paris), it proved to be a magnificent monument for the city's most popular artistic expression, the *bel canto*.

Building contractor-cum-impresario Angelo Carasale completed the work in just 300 days, carrying out Giovanni Antonio Medrano's opulent design in gold, silver and blue, the colours of the Bourbon royal household. To give the royal guests easy access to the theatre, it was built on to the Palazzo Reale. The backdrop could originally be opened out on to the palace gardens. With its 184 boxes arranged in six tiers, the San Carlo still seats an audience of 3,000, making it one of Europe's largest opera houses.

In 1810, in keeping with the French taste of the time, Napoleon's Joachim Murat had Tuscan architect Antonio Niccolini add a new neo-classical façade. Destroyed by fire six years later, it was faithfully rebuilt by Niccolini for the Bourbon King Ferdinand. Composers Rossini and Donizetti both wrote and conducted operas for the San Carlo, and in 1835 Donizetti directed the world première of his hyper-romantic tragedy, *Lucia di Lammermoor*. The guided tour will show you the architecture, but only a performance can convey the essential fourth dimension, the fervent Neapolitan audience.

**www.**teatrosancarlo.it

🍴 19J ✉ Via San Carlo 98/f ☎ 081 797 2331/2412/2312 🕐 Opera season Nov–Jun ✋ Opera very expensive; recitals expensive; guided tours moderate 🍴 Caffè Gambrinus (€€), restaurants near by (€€) 🚌 R2, R3 ❓ Daily tours outside rehearsal times; contact theatre bookshop, ☎ 081 400 300

## VILLA FLORIDIANA

The villa and its handsome gardens, now one of Naples' most attractive public parks, were designed in 1819 by Antonio Niccollini as a summer *palazzina* for Ferdinand Bourbon's wife, Lucia Migliaccio, Duchess of Floridia. Amid groves of oak, pine and lemon trees the neo-classical villa houses the **Museo Nazionale della Ceramica 'Duca di Martina'** which has an impressive collection of European, Chinese and Japanese ceramics. Placido de Sangro, Duke of Martina, was in the 1880s a passionate collector of all manner of *objets d'art* picked up on his travels around Europe – glassware, coral, bronzes – but, above all, it is his porcelain and majolica that make this museum outstanding. It ranges from Spanish–Moorish to Italian Renaissance, from finest German Meissen to French Sèvres, including one delightful piece from the Rambouillet palace dairy, a cup of unmistakable shape known as *Le sein de la Reine* (the Queen's Breast), without identifying the queen.

🔲 15K ✉ Via Domenico Cimarosa 77 ☎ 081 578 8418 🕐 Villa: Tue–Sun 8.30–1.30. Gardens: daily 8:30–dusk ✋ Villa: inexpensive. Gardens: free 🍴 Cafés and restaurants near by (€–€€) 🚇 Metro Piazza Vanvitelli, Funicolare (cable-car) di Chiaia

**Museo Nazionale della Ceramica 'Duca di Martina'**
☎ 081 578 8418 🕐 Thu–Tue 8.30–2, but hours and prices may vary according to temporary exhibitions

## HOTELS

### Canada (€–€€)
Overlooking Mergellina harbour, very simple but clean, air-conditioned three-star accommodation; 8 rooms with tiny baths. Convenient for hydrofoil to Capri.
✉ Via Mergellina 43 ☎ 081 680 952 🚇 Mergellina

### Cavour (€€)
Modern, well-run, family hotel by Stazione Centrale. Rooms are spacious and simply furnished with air-conditioning – ask for double-glazing (*con doppi vetri*). Good restaurant.
✉ Piazza Garibaldi 32 ☎ 081 283 122; www.hotelcavournapoli.it
🚇 Piazza Garibaldi

### Excelsior (€€€)
A grand hotel; magnificent roof-garden view of Castel dell'Ovo.
✉ Via Partenope 44 ☎ 081 764 0111; www.excelsior.it 🚌 3

### Pinto Storey (€€)
Fashionable location behind Villa Pignatelli. Rooms tastefully furnished; impeccable bedlinen and bathrooms; friendly service. Lovely breakfast room.
✉ Via Giuseppe Martucci 72 ☎ 081 681 260; www.pintostorey.it 🚌 R3

### Rex (€€)
Rex is in a restored *palazzo* that has original ceiling paintings and art nouveau décor. Bright, colourful rooms, double-glazed and air-conditioned.
✉ Via Palepoli 12 ☎ 081 764 9389; www.hotelrex.it 🚌 R3

### Santa Lucia (€€€)
Renovated neo-classical seafront hotel. Elegant, spacious and comfortable rooms. Breakfast buffet a major attraction.
✉ Via Partenope 46 ☎ 081 764 0666; www.santalucia.it 🚌 R3

### Soggiorno Sansevero (€)
Under same management as Albergo, this boarding house

occupies part of the legendary Sansevero princes' *palazzo*. Private baths in four of six clean, comfortable rooms. Breakfast in famous Scaturchio Café included.

✉ Piazza San Domenico Maggiore 9 ☎ 081 551 5949; www.albergosansevero.it 🚌 R1

### Vesuvio (€€€)

Ultimate luxury hotel. Opulently furnished rooms; bay view. Enrico Caruso left his name on the most luxurious suite, the rooftop restaurant, and a pasta dish.

✉ Via Partenope ☎ 081 764 004; www.vesuvio.it 🚌 R3

### Villa Capodimonte (€€€)

A modern but stylishly decorated establishment in a tranquil hillside location near Capodimonte Museum and park. Terrace restaurant.

✉ Via Moiariello 66 ☎ 081 459 000; www.villacapodimonte.it 🚌 110

## RESTAURANTS

### Bellini (€–€€)

In the student district with shady terrace. Popular up-market pizzeria and good all-round trattoria. Try house Pizza Bellini (mozzarella, ham and mushrooms), seafood pasta or fine grilled fish.

✉ Via Santa Maria di Costantinopoli 79–80 ☎ 081 459 774 🕔 Closed Sun, 10 days in mid-Aug 🚌 R1, R4

### Brandi (€–€€)

Having created the flagship Pizza Margherita in 1889 (P36), this venerable pizzeria still attracts crowds. Try, too, *pizza all'ortolana* (garden vegetables) or *pescatora* (seafood). Delicious rum baba.

✉ Salita Sant'Anna di Palazzo 1 (behind Piazza Trieste e Trento) ☎ 081 416 928 🕔 Closed three days in mid-Aug 🚌 R2, R3

### La Caffettiera

See page 60.

### La Cantinella (€€€)

Elegant address near big Santa Lucia hotels. Exquisite service, fresh seafood and exceptional wine cellar attract Naples' high society. Seafood pasta *(pappardelle agli scampi* and *tagliatelle Santa Lucia)* and monkfish in seafood sauce *(rana pescatrice)* are house specialities. Pastry chef does wonders with citrus fruit.

✉ Via Cuma 42 ☎ 081 764 8684 🕓 Closed Sun, mid-Aug 🚌 R3

### Caruso (€€€)

Romantic views over the Bay of Naples and Castel dell' Ovo is the major appeal of this celebrated roof garden restaurant at the top of the Vesuvio hotel. Try maestro's *bucatini Enrico Caruso.*

✉ Grande Albergo Vesuvio, Via Partenope 45 ☎ 081 764 0520 🕓 Closed Mon 🚌 R3

### La Chiacchierata (€€)

Family trattoria near Piazza del Plebiscito, with Mamma Anna cooking and checking everybody is happy. Robust cuisine, lusty vegetable soups. Daily change of menu, so let Anna choose for you. *Chiacchierata* means 'chat'.

✉ Piazzetta Matilde Serao 37 ☎ 081 411 465 🕓 Mon–Thu lunch only, Fri, lunch and dinner, Sat lunch only. Closed Sun and Aug 🚌 R2, R3

### Al Cinquantatre (€€)

Long-established trattoria in *centro storico* with pleasant terrace. Traditional Neapolitan cooking attracts both local regulars and discerning foreign clientele. Big choice of *antipasti*; savoury speciality is *minestra maritata* soup, and lasagne is first rate.

✉ Piazza Dante 53 ☎ 081 549 9372 🕓 Daily 🚌 R1, R4

### Ciro a Santa Brigida (€€–€€€)

Run by the Pace family for over 100 years. Highest quality; subtle antipasti, old-fashioned *o pignatiello de vavella* (shellfish soup), seafood or vegetable pasta, and *pizza d'oro*, with whole cherry tomatoes.

✉ Via Santa Brigida 72, near Galleria Umberto I ☎ 081 552 4072 🕓 Closed Sun in summer 🚌 R2

### Gambrinus
See page 60.

### Giuseppone a Mare (€€–€€€)
One of Naples' top seafood restaurants with a grand bay view. Fresh fish, *tagliatelle al tartufo e asparagi* (truffles and asparagus), and *linguine al nero* (in squid ink). Good wines, rich choice of desserts.

✉ Via Ferdinando Russo 13, Capo Posillipo ☎ 081 769 1384 🕔 Closed Sun dinner, Mon, Aug, Christmas 🚌 C21

### Intra Moenia
See page 60.

### Masaniello (€€)
In the stableblock of an old *palazzo* in *centro storico*, you can expect to find traditional Neapolitan dishes and great pizzas – especially with *rucola* (rocket) or *salsiccie* (sausage).

✉ Via Donnalbina 28 (behind Santa Maria La Nova church) ☎ 081 552 8863 🕔 Closed Sun, few days Aug 🚌 R1

### Di Matteo (€)
Di Matteo was Spaccanapoli's best-loved pizzeria long before President Bill Clinton visited in 1994, but it's even more crowded now. Expect to have to queue, but it's worth the wait. The Margherita is the purists' choice, commonly eaten Neapolitan-style *a libretto* (folded in two).

✉ Via dei Tribunali 94 ☎ 081 455 262 🕔 Closed Sun, two weeks in Aug 🚇 Piazza Cavour

### Mimì Alla Ferrovia (€€–€€€)
Grand family institution with a reputation for fine food, sufficient to make people miss trains. Simplicity and finesse combine in *pasta e fagioli* (noodles and beans) and famous *linguine al Mimi* (scampi, shrimp, scallops) and plain fennel salad.

✉ Via Alfonsa d'Aragona 21 ☎ 081 553 8525 🕔 Closed Sun, week in mid-Aug 🚇 Piazza Garibaldi

### Osteria Castello (€)

A modest family trattoria in fashionable Chiaia serving fine *bucatini all'amatriciana* (pasta with ham and red bell-peppers), pepper steaks and good home-made desserts.

✉ Via Santa Teresa a Chiaia 38 ☎ 081 400 486 🕐 Closed Sun, Aug 🚌 R3

### La Sacrestia (€€€)

Overlooking the bay from Posillipo, this is one of Naples' most prestigious restaurants. The menu includes exquisite aubergine (eggplant) ravioli, delicate *fagottini* (pasta rolls with chives, ricotta and spinach), fresh fish and an excellent wine list.

✉ Via Orazio 116 ☎ 081 761 1051 🕐 Closed Aug 🚌 C21

### Scaturchio

See page 61.

### Taverna dell'Arte (€€)

With tasteful and romantic décor, this fine old trattoria in the *centro storico* serves typical Neapolitan dishes: *minestra maritata* soup, stuffed pork, a great variety of vegetables and local wines.

✉ Rampa San Giovanni Maggiore 1a ☎ 081 552 7558 🕐 Dinner only. Closed Sun 🚌 R2

## SHOPPING

### Aldo Tramontano

Renowned for its *haute couture* leather goods.

✉ Via Chiaia 143 ☎ 081 414 758 🚌 R2, R3

### Antiche Delizie

Wonderful delicatessen, with outstanding cheese, meats and wines.

✉ Via Pasquale Scura 14 ☎ 081 551 3088 🚌 24, 105, R1

### Bowinkel

Wonderful collection of Naples prints, bronzes, fans, costumes.

✉ Piazza dei Martiri 24 ☎ 081 764 4344 🚌 R2, R3

### Brinkmann

Meticulously handcrafted jewellery.

✉ Piazza Municipio 21 ☎ 081 552 0108 or 081 551 6733. (Also at Via Bisignano 9, 081 405 639/403 940) 🚍 R2, R3

### Caso

Highly reputed for its antique jewels, vintage watches and delicate coralware.

✉ Piazza San Domenico Maggiore 16 ☎ 081 552 0108/551 6733

### Coin

Excellent for one-stop shopping with a sophisticated range of goods.

✉ Via Scarlatti 98–100 ☎ 081 578 0111

### Feltrinelli

Naples' best all-round bookshop with range of English-language literature.

✉ Via San Tommaso d'Aquino 70/76 ☎ 081 552 1436; www.lafeltrinelli.it 🚍 R2, R3

### Fiera Antiquaria

Antiques fair in municipal park two weekends a month.

✉ Viale Anton Dohrn, Villa Comunale ☎ 081 761 2541 🚍 R2, R3

### Guida

Matchless selection of second-hand and rare books.

✉ Via Port'Alba 20/23 ☎ 081 446 377 🚍 R1, R4

### Marinella

Made-to-measure ties for celebrities, heads of state and VIPs.

✉ Riviera di Chiaia 287 ☎ 081 245 1182 🚍 R2, R3

### Pignasecca Flea Market

Occasional antiques turn up among the usual bric-à-brac.

✉ Off Piazza Carità 🚍 R1, R4

### La Rinascente

Quality clothes, perfumes and household goods.

✉ Via Toledo 340 ☎ 081 411 511

### Scaturchio

Historic pastry shop famous for its *sfogliatelle* and house specialities; *zeffiro all'arancia* (orange delicacy), and chocolate and rum *ministeriale*.

✉ Piazza San Domenico Maggiore 19 ☎ 081 551 6944

### Treves

Good selection of Italian and international novels.

✉ Via Toledo 249/250 ☎ 081 415 211 🚍 R1, R4

## ENTERTAINMENT

## CLASSICAL MUSIC

### Auditorium RAI-TV

The national TV network's concert hall stages both classical music and jazz.

✉ Via Guglielmo Marconi (Fuorigrotta) ☎ 081 725 1506/1111 (RAI switchboard)

### Bellini

Only recently resumed, with both drama and operatic productions.

✉ Via Conte di Ruvo 17 ☎ 081 549 9688; www.teatrobellini.it 🚍 R1

### Conservatorio San Pietro a Majella

Housed since 1826 in a handsome 14th-century convent, the Music Conservatory has two concert halls, the Alessandro Scarlatti for orchestral concerts and the smaller Giuseppe Martucci for chamber music recitals.

✉ Via San Pietro a Majella 35 ☎ www.sanpeitroamajella.it 🚍 R1

### Teatro delle Palme

Chamber music recitals are staged here by the Associazione Scarlatti.

✉ Via Vetriera 12 ☎ 081 418 134 🚍 R3

### Teatro San Carlo

One of the world's most beautiful opera houses (► 104–105), the theatre stages opera, ballet and symphonic concerts played by its resident Orchestra Sinfonica and guest orchestras. The season runs from November to June.

✉ Via San Carlo 98/F ☎ 081 797 2331/2412/2314 🚌 R2, R3

### CLUBS

The city's club scene changes fast. Chiaia's Piazza dei Martiri is a mob scene, Piazza Bellini lively but more sedate. *Qui Napoli* publishes up-to-date listings, but here are a few 'institutions'.

### Around Midnight

A friendly and long-established jazz club and bar.

✉ Via Giuseppe Bonito 32/9 ☎ 081 558 2834

### Madison Street

Naples' biggest disco caters to a trendy crowd attracted by the different theme nights – gay on Saturday.

✉ Via Sgambati 47 ☎ 081 546 4930

### La Mela

More elegant than most in the fashionable Chiaia district.

✉ Via dei Mille 40 ☎ 081 410 270

# Bay of Naples

**The beauty of the Bay of Naples is almost too perfect – the bold curve around the city itself, the romantic profile of Mount Vesuvius, and beyond, the rugged Sorrento peninsula, all flanked by the sentinel islands of Capri and Ischia.**

Despite the vaporous fumaroles of the Campi Flegrei to the west and the urban monstrosities around the ancient ruins of Pompei and Herculaneum to the east, beauty prevails. Away from the metropolitan sprawl, the clear coastal waters are suffused with the bay's unique luminosity to produce truly emerald green and sapphire blue grottoes. And the splendours of Roman antiquity survive, from the Pompeian houses and shops to the imperial villas of Capri.

# Capri

Capri – age cannot wither her nor package tours stale her infinite variety. The colours and fragrance of Mediterranean and subtropical vegetation, elegant patrician villas, romantic Roman ruins amid mountain greenery, overlooking blue waters washing over secluded coves and mysterious grottoes – all seduce the willing visitor. Emperor Tiberius was charmed into building 12 villas here; an heir to the Krupp steel fortune turned away from the family business; and countless painters and poets have forgotten to go home.

Hydrofoils and ferries serve Capri from Naples, Sorrento and Positano. Naples' hydrofoil takes 35 minutes, the cheaper ferry 80 minutes, but with the latter you get the chance to see dolphins pilot the boat across the bay and, for newcomers, a more charming first view of the island from the deck.

**www.**capritourism.com

270 Marina Grande-Capri; Marina Grande-Anacapri; Capri-Anacapri; Anacapri-Grotta Azzurra Caremar (Naples, Sorrento, Positano) 199 123 199; www.caremar.it Capri permits personally owned cars year round, hire cars from 1 Nov to 1 April. Best form of transport is the local bus or boat

## ANACAPRI

The island's second (Ana- means 'other'), quieter town, with white houses halfway up the slopes of Monte Solaro, is served by a scenic chairlift from Piazza Vittoria. Via Capodimonte, lined with tourist shops, leads to Villa San Michele (➤ 118). On Piazza San Nicola, the baroque church of San Michele has majolica-tiled paving showing the *Garden of Eden* (1761) by Francesco Solimena.

➕ 27Q

**Chairlift** 🏂 Mar–Oct 9:30 to one hour before sunset; Nov–Apr 10.30–3. Closed Tue in winter ☎ 081 837 1428 💵 Moderate

ℹ Via Giuseppe Orlandi 59 ☎ 081 837 1524

## GROTTA AZZURRA

See pages 38–39.

## PARCO AUGUSTO AND VIA KRUPP

The Parco Augusto, at the southern edge of Capri Town, offers splendid panoramas over the Certosa di San Giacomo, the harbour of Marina Piccola and the great Faraglioni rocks out in the bay. Just right of the gardens is a bust of Lenin, who visited his writer friend Maxim Gorky's villa in 1910. Starting under the park's bridge, the spectacular Via Krupp winds dizzily down to the sea with magnificent coastal views on the way. It was built by Friedrich Alfred Krupp (1854–1902), playboy son of a steel magnate who was believed to have committed suicide when accused of organizing orgies in an island grotto.

➕ 27Q ✉ Via Matteotti 🏂 Daily 9 to one hour before sunset

## VILLA JOVIS

Best preserved of Emperor Tiberius's villas on Capri, this grand residence sprawls across the island's eastern promontory. Built around three vast cisterns for storing rainwater, the imperial apartments are on the north side, bathhouses to the south, and servants' quarters to the west. The view across the bay to

Vesuvius was the emperor's parting gift to enemies hurled over the precipice known as Salto di Tiberio (Tiberius Jump). **www.**villajovis.it

➕ 27Q ✉ Via Tiberio ☎ 081 837 0634 ⏰ Daily 9 to one hour before sunset. Closed Jan 1, Easter Sun, Jun 2, Aug 15, Dec 25 💵 Inexpensive

## VILLA SAN MICHELE

A short walk from Anacapri's Piazza Vittoria, this villa is a charming monument to Axel Munthe (1857–1949), Swedish author of *The Story of San Michele*. Built by the writer-physician himself, the house is an eclectic mix of styles, combining baroque furnishings and Roman antiquities. It grew out of a villa and chapel which themselves stand on ruins from the Roman era.

➕ 27Q ✉ Viale Axel Munthe 3 ☎ 081 837 1401 ⏰ May–Sep 9–6; Apr and Oct 9.30–5; Mar 9.30–4.30; Nov–Feb 10.30–3.30 💵 Moderate

# What to See in the Bay of Naples

## CAMPI FLEGREI AND THE SPA TOWNS

Volcanic activity in the Phlegrean (Greek for 'burning') Fields fascinated ancient Romans and later European aristocrats on the Grand Tour. They came hoping for a (mild) eruption and to bathe in the hot springs. Agnano Terme has spa facilities built into caves next to the crater of an extinct volcano – and within the crater there is weekend horseracing at the **Ippodromo**. Growing in another crater, just to the north, are the Astroni woodlands once used by King Alfonso of Aragon for hunting, they are now a nature reserve. Pozzuoli, originally a Greek trading port (in the 6th century bc), is the region's largest town and has a large **Roman amphitheatre**. In the slumbering **Solfatara** crater on the eastern outskirts, with mudpools and sulphurous fumaroles.

Baia and Bacoli remain the fashionable seaside resorts they were for ancient Romans. One attraction is the ruin of an imperial villa in Baia's **Parco Archeologico.** Cuma, one of the western Mediterranean's oldest Greek colonies (750BC), has romantic ruins overgrown with vines, two Greek temples, a Roman forum and the Antro della Sibilla (Cave of the Cumaean Sybil), from which the prophetess dispensed her wisdom.

➕ 27S 🍴 Pozzuoli, Bacoli, Baia (€–€€) 🚆 Ferrovia Cumana from Montesanto (Naples) 🚹 Via Campi Flegrei, 3 Pozzuoli ☎ 081 526 1481/9198

**Ippodromo di Agnano**

🕐 Jun–Sep, Sat, Sun first race 8pm; Oct–May, Sat, Sun first race 3pm

**Anfiteatro Flavio (Roman amphitheatre)**

✉ Via Terracciano 75, Pozzuoli ☎ 081 526 6007 🕐 Wed–Mon 9 to 1hr before sunset, closed Tue 🖐 Moderate

**Solfatara**

✉ Via Solfatara 161, Pozzuoli ☎ 081 526 2341 🕐 Daily 8:30 to 1hr before sunset 🖐 Inexpensive

**Parco Archeologico di Baia**

✉ Via Fusaro 35 ☎ 081 868 752 🕐 Daily 9 to 1hr before sunset 🖐 Cheap

## HERCULANEUM

In an enclosure within the modern town of Ercolano, Herculaneum is less immediately spectacular than Pompei (➤ 128–131), but more compact and generally better preserved. Even a short visit gives a clear idea of what an ancient Roman town looked like. Whereas the eruption of AD79 destroyed Pompei with volcanic cinders, it buried Herculaneum under rivers of hot mud, creating a protective crust up to 20m (65ft) thick. Houses survived with one and even two upper storeys and woodwork intact, though they were stripped of paintings by Bourbon excavators in the 18th century. The excavated part – much, perhaps most, of the site is still buried under the modern town – suggests a leisured aristocratic community compared to more commercially oriented Pompei.

The town's grid plan runs south from its main street, Decumanus Maximus, to a promontory once much closer to the sea. The bay view made this a choice neighbourhood. The large Casa dei Cervi, House of the Stags (Cardus V), is named after its sculpture of stags being attacked by dogs. It also depicts a very drunk Hercules. On Cardus IV are impressive multiple family dwellings with two upper floors: Casa del Tramezzo di Legno (House of the Wooden Partition) and Casa Graticcio (Lattice House), with a balcony overlooking the street. Further north, Casa del Mobilo Carbonizzato (House of the Charred Furniture) retains a divan bed and a small table. Next door, the wine merchant's Casa di Nettuno (House of Neptune) has a miraculously preserved ground-floor counter, utensils, shelves of wine jars and, in its courtyard, a pretty green and blue mosaic of Neptune and his wife, Amphitrite.

✚ 28R ✉ Scavi (excavations), Corso Ercolano 123 ☎ 081 857 5347
⏰ Daily Apr–Oct 8.30–7.30 (last ticket 6); Nov–Mar 8.30–5 (last ticket 3.30). Closed Jan 1, May, Dec 25 ✋ Expensive 🍴 Cafés (€) near tourist office
🚆 Circumvesuviana (from Naples or Sorrento) to Ercolano ❓ Guided tours available ℹ Via IV Novembre 82 ☎ 081 788 1243

## ISCHIA

As Pithecusa (Monkey Island), Ischia was the Greek settlers' first Italian foothold (800BC) before they went on to colonize Cuma 50 years later (► 119). Geologically, the island is a volcanic extension of the Campi Flegrei (► 119) via the two stepping-stone isles of Procida and tiny Vivara, a nature reserve. The only volcanic activity apparent today is the hot springs, notable at the fashionable resorts of Casamicciola Terme and Lacco Ameno.

Lacco Ameno's modest little Museo Archeologico displays finds from the ancient Greek settlement, including 'Nestor's Cup' with the oldest known inscription of Greek verse, dating from the time that Homer's epics were first written down.

The main harbour town of Ischia Porto is a largely 18th-century development, with Terme Comunali (public spa facilities) just beyond the port. The late afternoon *passeggiata* takes place on Corso Vittoria Colonna, past the boutiques, cafés, restaurants and majolica-domed church of Santa Maria delle Grazie.

Fast-growing Forio is the most popular west coast resort, with its landmark silhouette of the gleaming white 16th-century Santuario del Soccorso. Just outside town, British composer Sir William Walton built his villa, **La Mortella,** which is famous for its garden planted with magnolia and palm trees.

➕ 26R 🚌 From major towns, island circuit 2.5 hours, CD buses clockwise, CS counter-clockwise 🚢 Hydrofoil from Naples (Molo Beverello) to Ischia Port or Forio, Alilauro ☎ 081 761 1004 🛈 Via Antonio Sogliuzzo 72 ☎ 081 507 4211

**La Mortella**

✉ Via F Calise 35, Forio ☎ 081 986 220; www.lamortella.it
🕐 Apr–Oct Tue, Thu, Sat, Sun 9–7 💰 Expensive

# a drive

# around the Sorrento Peninsula

This tour takes in the peninsula's rugged north coast, the plains of citrus groves and mountains of the interior, with spectacular views over both the Bay of Naples (➤ 115–138) and the west end of the Amalfi Coast (➤ 139–153).

*On the A3 autostrada from Naples, fork south to the Castellammare di Stabia exit to start the drive. From Castellammare's Villa Quisisana, S145 hairpins up Monte Faito before heading back down to the coast to Vico Equense.*

Castellammare di Stabia (ancient Stabiae) has been a renowned spa resort since Roman antiquity. It was buried by the Vesuvius eruption of AD79, but was quickly rebuilt. It has a medieval castle and the Antiquarium Stabiae exhibiting archaeological finds. On Monte Faito, woods of ash, chestnut and pine alternate with meadows, vineyards and olive groves. Earthquake and war destroyed all Vico Equense's historic treasures, apart from a Gothic church and medieval gate.

*From Vico, the road continues to Meta where it forks west to Sant'Agnello and Sorrento (➤ 132). At the west end of the ever-popular resort, S145 turns left up to Sant'Agata.*

For those not lunching in Sorrento, Sant'Agata sui due Golfi is home to one of Italy's most prestigious – and expensive – gourmet restaurants (Don Alfonso, ➤ 137–138) plus, absolutely free, a magnificent view over both the Bay of Naples and the Bay of Salerno.

*From Sant'Agata an optional detour down to the peninsula's south coast at Marina di Cantone will add a 45-minute drive each way before continuing to the end of the drive at Positano (► 46–47).*

Marina di Cantone is a little beach resort much appreciated by the sailing fraternity for its seafood restaurants. The road east to Positano offers a first glimpse of the charms of the Amalfi Coast.

**Distance** 85–110km (53–68 miles), depending on detours
**Time** Allow a day
**Start point** Castellamare di Stabia ✚ 29R
**End point** Positano ✚ 29Q
**Lunch** O'Parrucchiano (€–€€) ✉ Corso Italia 71, Sorrento
☎ 081 878 1321

## POMPEI

This is the stuff of ancient Roman daily life. We are its privileged witnesses today, thanks to the town's tragic burial under volcanic ash in AD79 and its miraculous preservation until excavations began in 1748. Along with its temples, town hall, theatres and other public buildings, the shops and houses are still here, the market, the bakery and brothel, the wine shop and grocery store – and poignant remains of people trapped in the catastrophe. Once located much closer to the sea than it is today, at the mouth of the Sarno River, Pompei prospered as a distribution centre for farming produce – wheat, olives, table grapes and wine – from the surrounding communities. Its population was perhaps 20,000 to 30,000.

The visit divides conveniently into public buildings and private houses. Original frescoes and sculptures are still in place, but some are exhibited in Naples' Museo Archeologico (► 42–43).

The Forum is directly up the road from the Porta Marina

entrance. Left and right of the entrance to the main square is a temple to Apollo and a basilica housing the chamber of commerce and the courthouse. The Forum was flanked on three sides by two-storey porticoes of Doric and Ionic columns. At the south end, in front of the municipal offices, are plinths for statues of politicians, and a white platform for orators. At the far end is the six-columned Capitolium (shrine) dedicated to Jupiter, Juno and Minerva. In the northeast corner, the porticoed Macellum was the town's main fish, meat and vegetable market.

Via della Abbondanza was a busy thoroughfare leading east from the south end of the Forum; the curved stone paving is rutted by chariot wheels and has raised pedestrian crossings. The walls are scratched or daubed in red with ancient graffiti – insults, obscene drawings, advertising and election campaign slogans. To the left, on Vico Lupanare (Brothel Alley) is one of Pompeii's 25 registered brothels, a two-storey building with naughty frescoes.

The Terme Stabiane (Stabian Baths), back on Via della Abbondanza, are built around a porticoed *palaestra* (gymnasium) with a swimming pool to the left. On the right, beyond the vestibule, men undressed in the *apodyterium* and went from *tepidarium* (warm) to *caldarium* (hot) rooms before cooling off in the *frigidarium*. The women's baths are beyond the furnaces north of the *caldarium*.

The Teatro Grande seated 5,000 spectators to watch the plays of Plautus and Terence, and also gladiators whose *caserma* (barracks) were behind the stage in the large *quadriporticus* (rectangular building). The smaller, originally roofed, Teatro Piccolo probably staged concerts and poetry recitals.

Of the surviving private houses, three north of the Forum stand out. Casa dei Vettii, belonging to two wealthy ex-slaves, is built around two sides of a columned, peristyle garden. A bold priapic figure in the entrance hall is just the first of many superb wall-paintings. The palatial Casa del Fauno is named after the bronze faun statue in its courtyard, brought to Pompei from Alexandria in the 2nd century BC. It has fine mosaics, a majestic colonnade and a formal garden planted with shrubs common in antiquity. Casa del Poeta Tragico is famous for its threshold mosaic, a fierce chained dog and the timeless inscription *Cave Canem* (Beware of the Dog).

✚ 29R ✉ Pompei Scavi, Porta Marina ☎ 081 861 0744 🕓 Daily Apr–Oct 8.30–7.30 (last ticket 6); Nov–Mar 8.30–5 (last ticket 3.30). Closed Jan 1, May, Dec 25 🎫 Expensive: ticket includes main site and Villa dei Misteri (➤ 52–53) 🍽 Pleasant cafeteria (€) near the Forum 🚉 Circumvesuviana: Pompei–Scavi (Villa dei Misteri) ❓ English-language tours with official guides; maps for self-guided tours from ticket office ℹ Via Sacra 1 ☎ 081 850 8451 or 081 850 7255

## SORRENTO

The clifftop resort, which enjoyed a heyday in the 19th century, remains popular as a base from which to explore the Sorrento peninsula and beyond. Sitting on a natural terrace with a sheer drop to the sea and ravines on either side, the town is surrounded by lovely gardens. Its name is linked by legend to the sirens who tried to lure Ulysses and his sailors on to the rocks below.

Named after the town's illustrious 16th-century poet Torquato Tasso, Piazza Tasso is the gateway to Sorrento's *centro storico* (historic centre). A major monument here is the art nouveau Grand Hotel Vittoria, with ancient marble columns in its gardens left from its predecessor, the villa of Emperor Augustus. Medieval Via Pietà leads to the heart of the old town past the 13th-century Byzantine-style Palazzo Veniero (No.14) and 15th-century Palazzo Correale (No.24), now part of the baroque Santa Maria della Pietà.

Across from the campanile of the cathedral, Via Giuliani leads to the Sedile Dominova. This 15th-century arcaded loggia, where the town's nobles held their council, is today a club for card-players.

The **Museo Correale di Terranova** houses a family collection of Greek and Roman antiquities, Neapolitan painting and European porcelain, glass and clocks.

✚ 28Q 🚌 Naples Capodichino airport bus; SITA for Amalfi Coast
🚆 Circumvesuviana from Naples (Corso Garibaldi) 🛥 Hydrofoil from Naples Alilauro ☎ 081 497 2222 Sorrento hydrofoil to Capri and Amalfi Coast
☎ 081 807 1812 🛈 Via Luigi De Maio 35 ☎ 081 807 4033/877 3397

**Museo Correale di Terranova**

✉ Via Correale 48 ☎ 081 878 1846 🕐 Daily 9–2. Closed Tue and public hols 🖐 Expensive

## VESUVIUS (MONTE VESUVIO)

See pages 40–41.

## VILLA DEI MISTERI

See pages 52–53.

# a walk

# Sorrento to Massa Lubrense

This is a scenic walk with stunning panoramic views over the Bay of Sorrento and the hills. It is uphill and quite steep for most of the way and a little isolated in some spots. Don't attempt it in intense heat and take plenty of water.

*From Piazza Tasso take the Via Casareo, a narrow cobbled street. Towards the end of the road, after about 0.5km, is the Church of SS Annunziata on the left. At the end of the road turn right, then left at the parking sign, which leads to the restaurant Zi'ntonio Mare. There is a*

*slightly sloping road with a sheer rock face in front. Go along the high-walled path which narrows and becomes a tight passage between two houses, one yellow and one pink. Walk up the steps, go around the railing, and you will find yourself on the busy main road. At the International Camping sign a bit further on the right, turn left up the steep cobbled road and look back to admire the view over the bay. Negotiate the bends by taking the three paths that act as a shortcut. The road curves left, but go straight over to Via Priora, which takes you across a main*

road (beware of scooters). Carry on up to a shrine of the Madonna and Child and fork left into a trail in the middle of vineyards and lemon groves. Continue on for another 400m (0.25 miles) to a crossroads and beyond to join Via Bagnulo. Pass under the arch under the white house, take the first right and go down around two bends to a T-junction. Go left and then first right to Massa Lubrense's Church of Santa Maria Delle Grazie on Largo del Vescovado.

Frequent buses and taxis run back to Sorrento.

**Distance** 4km (2.5 miles) one way
**Time** 90 minutes one way, 3 hours round trip
**Start point** Piazza Tasso, Sorrento ✚ 28Q 🚌 SITA bus from Amalfi Coast
**End point** Largo del Vescovado, Massa Lubrense ✚ 28Q 🚌 SITA bus
**Lunch** Either in Sorrento or at Massa Lubrense, nothing en route. In Sorrento, The Red Lion (✉ via Marziale 25 ☎ 081 807 3089), despite its name, has typical local and national dishes at reasonable prices in a pub-like atmosphere. Meals start with a free tomato *bruschetta* and end with a free *limoncello* liqueur.

## HOTELS

### CAPRI
**Quisisana (€€€)**
Originally a high-class 19th-century sanatorium, now one of the world's best-known luxury hotels. Facilities include tennis, gym, indoor and outdoor swimming pools and two restaurants.
✉ Via Camerelle 2 ☎ 081 837 0788; www.quisi.com ⏱ Closed Nov–Mar

**Villa Krupp (€€€)**
Simple comfort in 12 rooms – originally home to Russian writer Maxim Gorky. Splendid view of Faraglioni rocks and Marina Piccola.
✉ Via Matteotti 12, near Parco Augusto ☎ 081 837 0362 ⏱ Closed Jan

### ISCHIA
**Villa Angelica (€–€€)**
Charming family villa in a quiet street on north coast.
✉ Via IV Novembre 28, Lacco Ameno ☎ 081 994 524; www.villaangelica.it
⏱ Closed Nov–15 April

## RESTAURANTS

### BACOLI
**Da Giona (€€)**
Beachfront seafood trattoria on the quiet cape west of Bacoli. Worth seeking out for the fish soup, pasta and *risotto frutti di mare* (seafood), and fresh fish, which are very good value.
✉ Via Dragonara 6, Capo Miseno ☎ 081 523 4659 ⏱ Closed Wed

### BAIA
**L'Altro Cucchiaro (€€€)**
One of Italy's finest seafood restaurants overlooking Baia's pretty harbour. Follow fresh *fritturine* (fried whitebait) with *gnocchi* or *spaghettini* in seafood sauce, or oven-baked *rana pescatrice* (monkfish). Terrific desserts.
✉ Via Lucullo 13, Baia Porto ☎ 081 868 7196 ⏱ Dinner only. Closed Sun, Mon, Aug

## CAPRI

### Aurora (€€)

In the heart of Capri old town. Traditional cooking: grilled vegetables, seafood pasta, the fresh catch of the day and great pizza.

✉ Via Fuorlavado 18 ☎ 081 837 0181 ◷ Closed Jan–Mar

### Gran Caffè

See page 60.

### Quisi (€€€)

Legendary hotel restaurant at legendary prices, but still providing the ultimate in luxury and refinement. Specialities include *fiorilli di zucca ripieni* (stuffed marrow), fish pâté, pasta with scampi and cherry tomatoes, *quaglia con castagne* (quail with chestnuts and foie gras).

✉ Grand Hotel Quisisana, Via Camerelle 2 ☎ 081 837 0788 ◷ Dinner only, Easter to Nov

### La Savardina da Edoardo

See page 61.

### Villa Brunella

See page 61.

## POZZUOLI

### Ludovico (€€)

An elegant restaurant that makes good use of the produce from the nearby fish market.

✉ Via Nicola Fasano 6 ☎ 081 526 8255 ◷ Closed Mon

## SANT'AGATA

### Don Alfonso (€€€)

One of southern Italy's most celebrated restaurants is in this pretty pink villa. The house specialities include *cipolla novella farcita* (spring onions stuffed with shrimp and bacon), *penne alle calamarette* (pasta with baby squid), *capretto lucano* (goat kid), and chocolate and wild cherry soufflé.

✉ Piazza Sant'Agata ☎ 081 878 0026 ⊘ Closed Mon; Tue in winter and a period during Feb–Mar

## SORRENTO
### O Parrucchiano
See page 60.

### Pollio
See page 60.

## SHOPPING

### La Campanina
An Aladdin's cave of elegantly mounted diamonds, sapphires and other stones, but also fine bracelets and necklaces.
✉ Via Vittorio Emanuele 18, Capri ☎ 081 837 0643

### Canfora
Famous since 1946 for handmade, classic shoes.
✉ Via Camerelle 3, Capri ☎ 081 837 0487; www.canfora.com

### Mennella
Traditional island craftwork, pottery and majolica tiling.
✉ Casamicciola Terme, Via Salvatore Girardi 47, Ischia ☎ 081 994 442

### Rosbenia
Bedlinen, tablecloths and napkins – all hand-embroidered in finest linen and lace.
✉ Piazza Angelina Laura 34, Sorrento ☎ 081 877 2341

### Siniscalco-Gori
Gallery of classical antiques and paintings, mostly 19th and early 20th century.
✉ Via Camerelle 89, Capri ☎ 081 837 6798

# The Amalfi Coast

**The rugged but never forbidding Costiera Amalfitana (Amalfi Coast) is one of Europe's happiest marriages of nature and civilization. The Lattari Mountains plunge to the Mediterranean, leaving little space for houses or roads, yet farmers have hewn terraces for vines, and olive and citrus trees join niches of wild rosemary, orchids, cyclamen and honeysuckle.**

The famous S163 highway somehow winds its way around curves and sudden hairpins. The town of Amalfi found a flat shelf at sea level from which to launch its maritime empire, while the houses of Positano hang on to the hillside, and Ravello withdrew inland, content with the coast's best view. Ruins of mountain lairs and lookout towers attest to the coast's turbulent past, a distant memory in the mellow present.

## AMALFI

The town's cosmopolitan atmosphere is not something new;
Amalfi's central position on the Bay of Salerno marked it out early
for a maritime destiny. Starting as a Byzantine protectorate in
AD839, it developed – along with Venice and well before Pisa and
Genoa – a commercial empire throughout the Mediterranean.

From the Arabs Amalfi acquired not only architectural models
for its duomo (cathedral) and Chiostro del Paradiso (➤ 37), but
also the nautical compass to gain a navigational headstart on its
rivals. In its 10th- and 11th-century heyday it had trading posts
from Tunis to Alexandria and Antioch, and was halted only by
the Normans.

From Piazza Duomo, explore the medieval arcades of Via dei
Mercanti (or Ruga Nova) from the foot of the cathedral campanile
to the Porta dell'Ospedale. The whitewashed passageway opens

out onto little gardens, the Church of Santa Maria Addolorata and the Capo de Ciuccio fountain. On the way are charming antique shops, wine merchants and shops specializing in the locally distilled *limoncello* (lemon liqueur), and potent fruity variations. A popular excursion, just 4km (2.5 miles) west of town, is to the **Grotta di Smeralda**, a cave where the waters are as brilliantly emerald green as those of Capri's Grotta Azzurra are sapphire blue.

🚌 29Q 🍴 Excellent cafés, pizzerias and restaurants around Piazza del Duomo (€–€€€) 🚌 SITA (from Naples, Sorrento and all coastal resorts) 🚤 Alicost hydrofoil and ferry ☎ 089 871 483 ❓ To beat the high season traffic, take the hydrofoil or ferry between Positano, Amalfi and Salerno 🛈 Corso Repubbliche Marinare 19 ☎ 089 871 107; www.amalficoastlines.com

### Grotta di Smeralda

✉ Statale 163, Conca dei Marini
🕐 Daily 9–4 💷 Moderate

## DUOMO DI AMALFI
See pages 36–37.

## PAESTUM

The admirably preserved Doric monuments of Paestum are among
the finest Greek temples anywhere – including Greece. The
temples are at last being liberated from their scaffolding after
years of meticulous restoration. Rising majestically from fields by
the sea, their honey-coloured stone columns bear witness to
Greek colonial prosperity in southern Italy, in particular Poseidonia,
as it was known before the Roman conquest in 273BC. This is
perhaps appropriate for a colony founded by traders from Sybaris,
whose taste for high living gave rise to the word 'sybarite'.

The temples, dating back to the 5th and 6th centuries BC, stood over the walled city's Roman forum and residential neighbourhoods. Scholars dispute the temples' modern names. At the southern end of the ancient city, the building with a nine-columned façade, mistakenly known as the Basilica, was more likely to have been a temple of Hera, the city's patron goddess. The interior's division in two by a central row of columns suggests worship of a second deity, perhaps Zeus. It was built around 530BC, about 100 years before its taller neighbour, Tempio di Nettuno (► 50–51). At the north end of the site, the discovery of Christian tombs suggests that the hexastyle (six-column façade) Temple of Athena, also mistakenly attributed to Ceres, was used as a church in the Middle Ages.

The **Museo Archeologico** exhibits Paestum's sculpture, ceramics and other works of art, most notably the Tomba del Tuffatore (Diver's Tomb) from the 5th century bc, a rare example of Greek mural painting.

32P · Via Magna Grecia · Daily 9 to one hour before sunset · Moderate (expensive if combining site and museum) · Nettuno (€–€€), Via Principe di Piemonte 2. Lunch only. Closed Mon in winter · 082 881 1028 · From Salerno, Piazza Concordia · Paestum on Salerno–Reggio di Calabria line · Guided tours; occasional lectures · Via Magna Grecia 151 · 082 881 1016

**Museo Archeologico**

82 881 1023 · Daily 9–7. Closed first and third Mon in the month

## POSITANO

See pages 46–47.

# a drive from Positano to Salerno

This is the famous Amalfi Drive along the coast road, taking in the 'Big Three' resorts: Positano (➤ 46–47), Amalfi (➤ 138–139) and Ravello (➤ 54–55). But on the way, it also offers a glimpse of smaller fishing villages and market towns such as Praiano, Atrani and Vietri, and briefly leaves the coastal highway after Amalfi for an incursion inland to look at the Lattari Mountains. It is particularly worthwhile going on to Salerno (➤ 148–149) if you are planning an excursion down to Paestum (➤ 142–143).

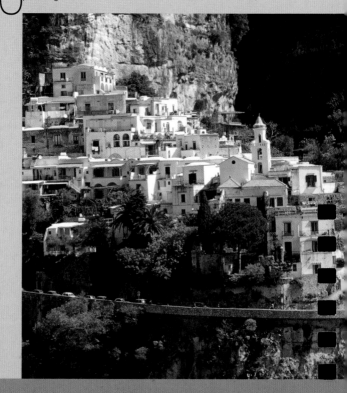

*From Positano, turn east and stay on the S163 until just after Amalfi, at Atrani. On this road more than most, keep well to the right and do not hesitate to use the horn on blind curves.*

Praiano's fishermen's houses are scattered across the ridge of Monte Sant'Angelo, and Marina di Praia is a charming little beach. Just before Conca dei Marini are signposts for the translucent green waters of the Grotta di Smeralda (➤ 141). Atrani is one of the coast's prettiest little towns, particularly on Piazza Umberto I.

*About 1km (0.5 miles) after Atrani, turn left at the Ravello exit. From the tunnel passing under Ravello, go left on the highway signposted Valico Chiunzi. Continue to the crossroads on the crest of the Lattari Mountain ridge, then turn right to take the highway back to the coast, signposted Maiori.*

This detour loops around the Tramonti plain, with some impressive rugged mountain views along the way. At this altitude, orange and lemon trees are replaced by vineyards and vegetable gardens with aubergines (eggplants), tomatoes and bell-peppers.

*At Maiori, turn left on to the S163 to continue via Vietri to Salerno.*

Vietri is famous for its majolica ceramics, both for domestic and monumental use. Notice the dome on the parish church of San Giovanni Battista.

**Distance** 70–80km (40–50 miles)
**Time** Take a whole day
**Start point** Positano 🚩 29Q **End point** Salerno 🚩 30R
**Lunch** Le Arcate (€–€€) ✉ Via G Di Benedetto 4, Atrani
☎ 089 871 367

## RAVELLO

About 350m (1,150ft) above Amalfi, the sumptuous villas of the town perch with aloof gentility among umbrella pines and lofty cypresses on a ridge flanked by the Dragone and Reginna valleys. Ancient Romans fled here from invading Visigoths and Huns; today, holidaymakers come to escape the crowds on the coast. Strolling around the magnificent gardens here and looking out to sea, along the cobbled lanes, it is easy to forget the outside world.

The medieval connection with the Duchy of Amalfi, and the lucrative role Ravello played in trade with Sicily, becomes clear both in the town's churches and its older villas, each showing the influence of Byzantine and Arab architectural styles – most notably the lovely Villa Rufolo (► 54–55), opposite the Duomo. The 11th-century cathedral has undergone heavy-handed baroque transformations, but its 13th-century campanile, with its handsome twin-mullioned windows, has the characteristic intertwining arches of Arab architecture. Inside the church, the richly decorated marble pulpit, borne aloft by six lions, captures the opulent style of the eastern Mediterranean. North of the Duomo, these elements reappear in the multiple-domed 12th-century Church of San Giovanni del Toro.

At the southern end of Ravello, the grandiose **Villa Cimbrone** was built in the 18th century and ingeniously incorporates ancient columns and medieval sculpture from the town's various churches and *palazzi*. Its splendid garden with a belvedere at the far edge of the Ravello ridge was landscaped by Lord Grimthorpe, designer of the clock mechanism for London's Big Ben.

✚ 29R 🍴 Cafés, restaurants (€–€€) around Piazza Duomo 🚌 SITA bus many times daily from Naples, hourly from Amalfi 6am–9pm ❓ Summer musical festival (► 24)

### Villa Cimbrone

✉ Via Santa Chiara 🕒 May–Sep 9–6pm; Oct–Apr 9am to sunset
✋ Moderate
ℹ Via Roma 18/bis ☎ 089 857 096; www.ravellotime.it

## SALERNO

The Allied army landings here in September 1943 made this key
industrial port the capital of liberated Italy for a few proud months.
But war – and earthquake – have destroyed much of what was
once an important university town, famous for its medical school
since the Middle Ages.

Today its historic centre has been reduced to a few narrow
lanes around the Via Portacatena, which extends through the
8th-century Arco di Arechi to the picturesque Via dei Mercanti.
There is a fine view of the old town from the Castello di Arechi,
which houses a museum of Salerno's history.

Salerno's magnificent cathedral was built in 1076 by the town's
Norman conqueror, Robert Guiscard. It underwent extensive
transformations in the 17th and 18th centuries, but with the rare
harmonious incorporation of existing architectural elements –

ancient Greek, Byzantine, Arab and Romanesque. Set in a neo-classical façade, the portal at the top of its stairway, the Porta dei Leoni, is adorned with Romanesque sculpted lions and an atrium with intertwining Arab arches supported by Greek columns from Paestum's temples. The monumental black doors were fashioned in Constantinople and set between classical Byzantine columns. But nothing is more lavish than the polychrome marble for the baroque crypt, rebuilt in the 17th century to house the supposed relics of the Apostle Matthew. Over the double altar are two bronze statues of the saint (1622). The next door museum contains an early medieval altar-front, embellished with 54 superb ivory panels.

✚ 30R 🚌 SITA from Naples and Amalfi Coast resorts 🚢 Hydrofoil from Positano, Amalfi (Alicost ☎ 089 871 483; www.amalficoastlines.com)
ℹ️ Via Roma 258 ☎ 089 224 744

## HOTELS

### AMALFI
**La Bussola (€–€€)**
Pleasant family hotel nicely situated on harbour promenade.
✉ Via Lungomare dei Cavalieri 16 ☎ 089 871 533; www.labussolahotel.it

**Villa Lara (€€)**
Intimate, six-room three-star hotel in garden setting with fine views.
✉ Via delle Cartiere 1 ☎ 089 873 6358; www.villalara.it

### POSITANO
**Casa Albertina (€€)**
Family hotel in classic Mediterranean house. Air-conditioned rooms are small but cosy.
✉ Via della Tavolozza 3 ☎ 089 875 143; www.casalbertina.com

**Sirenuse (€€€)**
One of southern Italy's finest hotels, run by an aristocratic family. Rooms are furnished with exquisite taste in traditional Mediterranean style. First-class restaurant and the coast's best swimming pool.
✉ Via Cristoforo Colombo 30 ☎ 089 875 066; www.sirenuse.it

### RAVELLO
**Palumbo (€€€)**
Opulent hotel occupying medieval Palazzo Confalone, which Wagner made his home while working on *Parsifal*. The spacious rooms have lovely garden views.
✉ Via San Giovanni del Toro 16 ☎ 089 857 244; www.hotelpalumbo.it

## RESTAURANTS

### AMALFI
**Da Gemma (€€€)**
Over 120 years old and still going strong in this elegant neighbourhood. Try the wonderfully rich fish soup, the *linguine*

*all'aragosta* (spiny lobster), or fresh fish, grilled or in white wine sauce. Da Gemma also has a fine wine cellar.

✉ Via Lorenzo d'Amalfi and Fra'Gerardo Sasso 10, near Piazza del Duomo
☎ 089 871 1345 🕐 Closed Wed in winter, and 15 Jan–15 Feb

### Da Maria (€€)

A delightful, friendly trattoria serving regional dishes, good fresh vegetables, varied *antipasti*, seafood pasta, the best of the local wines and great pizza.

✉ Via Lorenzo d'Amalfi 14, just off Piazza del Duomo ☎ 089 871 880
🕐 Closed Mon

## ATRANI
### Le Arcate (€–€€)

Come here for some excellent simple local dishes in a charming setting near the harbour in Atrani. There's good fresh seafood and friendly family service.

✉ Via G Di Benedetto 4 ☎ 089 871 367 🕐 Closed Mon except mid-Jun to Aug, and 15 Jan–15 Feb

## PAESTUM
### Nettuno (€–€€)

With its fine terrace view of Paestum's most beautiful temples (▶ 50–51), this smart trattoria serves honest regional cuisine, good pasta and risotto with excellent locally sourced seafood sauces.

✉ Via Principe di Piemonte ☎ 082 881 1028 🕐 Lunch only. Closed Mon off-season

## POSITANO
### La Buca di Bacco (€€–€€€)

Beachfront trattoria popular with families and yachters for snacks and sumptuous gourmet cuisine, fresh seafood and pastas.

✉ Via Rampa Teglia 8 ☎ 089 875 699 🕐 Closed Nov–Mar

### La Sponda (€€€)

Positano's finest food is exquisitely served in this luxurious but friendly family-run hotel. The cuisine is traditional but delicate and imaginative: seafood pasta and risotto, mixed grill of fresh fish and oven-baked local *pezzogna* fish. Fantastic rum baba or *torta di mandorla* (almond tart).

✉ Le Sirenuse Hotel, Via Cristoforo Colombo 30 ☎ 081 875 066
🕐 Daily all year

### La Zagara

See page 61.

### RAVELLO
### Cumpà Cosimo (€–€€)

Very popular with local residents as well as foreign celebrities (there are photos of Humphrey Bogart and Jackie Kennedy) for the unfailing quality of the pasta and seafood dishes, served in an agreeable atmosphere.

✉ Via Roma 44–46 ☎ 089 857 156 🕐 Closed Mon Nov–Feb

### Palumbo (€€€)

Palatial dining in the medieval Palazzo Confalone, now a luxury hotel, with superb terrace view of the Amalfi Coast. Try *insalata di seppioline* (baby squid with walnuts and celery), ravioli with mint (*menta*), *spigola all'arancia* (sea bass in orange sauce) and fine Ravello wines.

✉ Via San Giovanni del Toro 16 ☎ 089 857 244 🕐 Closed 6 Jan–15 Mar

## ENTERTAINMENT

### CLASSICAL MUSIC

At Christmas and in summer the resorts outside Naples stage classical concerts and recitals in the romantic setting of their medieval churches and historic villas.

### Convento di Santa Rosa

Just west of Amalfi, this 14th-century convent perched on a ridge above the Grotta di Smeralda (➤ 141) hosts summer concerts of chamber music. The organisers, Ravello Concert Society, also put on performances at Villa Rufolo (➤ 54–55).

✉ Via Roma, Conca dei Marini ☎ www.ravelloarts.org

### Villa Rufolo

The Amalfi Coast's most celebrated concerts are held in the gardens of Wagner's splendid 13th-century villa, where the German composer found the inspiration to write his opera Parsifal in 1877. The music, performed by major orchestras and conductors, is relayed through the streets of Ravello to create a magic atmosphere in keeping with his opera.

✉ Piazza del Vescovado, Ravello ☎ 089 858 422; www.ravellofestival.com

## CLUBS AND DISCOS

Clubbing in the coastal resorts seems surprisingly more restrained than in Naples. Some of the big hotels do a bit of desultory disco, often outside on the terrace. However, only a handful of places to dance at least some of the night away can be recomended. All open around 10pm and go on much later than the hotels.

## SPORT

### SAILING

The Bay of Naples' major sporting event is Capri's international regatta held in May. Regional regattas may be held in summer at the major Amalfi Coast resorts – and Naples, too. For details, check with the tourist information offices at Positano, Amalfi and Naples.

# Index

# Acknowledgements

The Automobile Association would like to thank the following photographers, companies and picture libraries for their assistance in the preparation of this book.

Abbreviations for the picture credits are as follows – (t) top; (b) bottom; (c) centre; (l) left; (r) right; (AA) AA World Travel Library.

**6/7** Spanish Quarter, AA/M Jourdan; **8/9** Fishing boat, AA/M Jourdan; **10t** Pompei, AA/M Jourdan; **10c** Moped, AA/M Jourdan; **10/11** Caserta Palace Gardens, AA/M Jourdan; **11tl** Street scene, AA/M Jourdan; **11tr** Castel dell' Ovo, AA/M Jourdan; **11cr** Nuns, AA/M Jourdan; **11b** Local men, AA/M Jourdan; **12t** Fish Market, AA/M Jourdan; **12b** Fruit and vegetable stall, AA/M Jourdan; **12/3t** Seafood, AA/M Jourdan; **13c** Food shop, AA/M Jourdan; **13b** Pizza, AA/C Sawyer; **14tl** Seafood, AA/T Souter; **14cl** Cooking pizza, AA/M Jourdan; **14br** Sardines, AA/T Souter; **14/5t** Lorry, AA/M Jourdan; **14/5b** Meat and cheese stall, AA/M Jourdan; **15** Coffee, AA/M Jourdan; **16/7t** Pizza, AA/C Sawyer; **16/7b** Café, AA/M Jourdan; **18tl** Villa Cimbrone, AA/M Jourdan; **18bl** Museo di Capodimonte, AA/M Jourdan; **18tr** Via San Gregorio Armeno, AA/M Jourdan; **19t** Amalfi Coast, AA/M Jourdan; **19c** Pompei, AA/C Sawyer; **19b** Sorrento, AA/M Jourdan; **20/1** Moped, AA/M Jourdan; **24** Easter Parade, AA/M Jourdan; **25** Pizza, AA/M Jourdan; **26t** Policewoman, AA/M Jourdan; **26b** Scooter, AA/M Jourdan; **27** Naples Central Station, AA/M Trewlawny; **28** Policeman, AA/M Jourdan; **30** Telephone box, AA/M Jourdan; **31** Post box, AA/M Jourdan; **33** Policeman, AA/M Jourdan; **34/5** Gardens at the Museo di Capodimonte, AA/M Jourdan; **36** Detail of a door at the Duomo di Amalfi, AA/M Jourdan; **36/7** Duomo di Amalfi, AA/M Jourdan; **38/9** Grotto Azzurra, World Pictures; **40/1** Monte Vesuvio, AA/T Souter; **41** Eruption of Vesuvius, AA; **42/3** Museo Archeologico di Napoli, Robert Harding Picture Library; **44** Museo di Capodimonte; AA/M Jourdan; **44/5** Museo di Capodimonte, AA/M Jourdan; **46** Positano, AA/M Jourdan; **46/7t** Ceramic plates, AA/M Jourdan; **46/7b** Positano, AA/M Jourdan; **48/9** Naples, AA/M Jourdan; **50/1** Tempio di Nettuno, AA/T Souter; **52/3** Villa dei Misteri in Pompei, Robert Harding Picture Library; **54/5** Villa Rufolo, AA/M Jourdan; **56/7** Pompei, AA/M Jourdan; **58/9** Coffee shop, AA/M Jourdan; **60/1** Restaurant, AA/M Jourdan; **62** Kayaking, AA/D Miterdiri; **65** Via Tribunali, AA/M Jourdan; **66/7** Positano, AA/M Jourdan; **68** Via San Gregorio Armeno, AA/M Jourdan; **70/1** Santa Chiara, AA/M Jourdan; **72** Pompei, AA/M Jourdan; **75** Palazzo Reale, AA/M Jourdan; **76** Ice cream, AA/S McBride; **78/9** Palazzo Reale, AA/M Jourdan; **80/1** Naples, AA/M Jourdan; **83** Via San Gregorio Armeno, AA/M Jourdan; **84/5** Castel Nuovo, AA/M Jourdan; **86/7** Castel Nuovo, AA/M Jourdan; **88** Certosa di San Martino, AA/M Jourdan; **90/1** Via San Gregorio Armeno, AA/M Jourdan; **91** Via San Gregorio Armeno, AA/M Jourdan; **92/3** Duomo, AA/M Jourdan; **94/5** Galleria Umberto I, AA/M Jourdan; **96/7** Palazzo Reale, AA/M Jourdan; **98/9** San Domenico Maggiore, AA/M Jourdan; **99** San Domenico Maggiore, AA/M Jourdan; **100** Santa Chiara, AA/M Jourdan; **100/1** Santa Chiara, AA/M Jourdan; **102** Castel dell'Ovo, AA/M Jourdan; **102/3** Santa Lucia, AA/M Jourdan; **104/5** Teatro San Carlo, CuboImages srl/Alamy; **106** Villa Floridiana, AA/M Jourdan; **115** Bay of Naples, AA/M Jourdan; **116** Capri, World Pictures; **118** Capri, World Pictures; **120** Herculaneum, AA/M Jourdan; **122/3** Herculaneum, AA/M Jourdan; **124/5** Ischia, World Pictures; **127** Sorrento, AA/C Sawyer; **128/9** Pompei, AA/M Jourdan; **130t** Pompei, AA/M Jourdan; **130b** Pompei, AA/M Jourdan **130/1** Pompei, AA/M Jourdan; **133** Sorrento, AA/C Sawyer; **134** Countryside near Massa Lubrense, AA/M Jourdan; **135** Building near Massa Lubrense, AA/M Jourdan; **139** Ravello, AA/M Jourdan; **140/1** Amalfi, AA/T Souter; **141t** Amalfi, AA/M Jourdan; **141b** Duomo di Amalfi, AA/C Sawyer; **142/3** Paestum, AA/T Souter; **144** Positano, AA/M Jourdan; **146** Ravello, AA/M Jourdan; **148/9** Salerno, AA/M Trelawny.

Every effort has been made to trace the copyright holders, and we apologise in advance for any accidental errors. We would be happy to apply the corrections in the following edition of this publication.

# Street Index

157

# Dear Reader

**Your comments, opinions and recommendations are very important to us. So please help us to improve our travel guides by taking a few minutes to complete this simple questionnaire.**

*You do not need a stamp (unless posted outside the UK). If you do not want to cut this page from your guide, then photocopy it or write your answers on a plain sheet of paper.*

*Send to:* **The Editor, AA World Travel Guides, FREEPOST SCE 4598, Basingstoke RG21 4GY.**

**Your recommendations...**

We always encourage readers' recommendations for restaurants, nightlife or shopping – if your recommendation is used in the next edition of the guide, we will send you a **FREE AA Guide** of your choice from this series. Please state below the establishment name, location and your reasons for recommending it.

_____
_____
_____
_____
_____

Please send me **AA Guide** _____

**About this guide...**

Which title did you buy?

AA _____

Where did you buy it? _____

When? m m / y y

Why did you choose this guide? _____
_____
_____
_____

Did this guide meet your expectations?

Exceeded ☐   Met all ☐   Met most ☐   Fell below ☐

Were there any aspects of this guide that you particularly liked? _____
_____
_____
_____

*continued on next page...*

*Victoria + James*
*Salvatone*

Is there anything we could have done better? _____
_____
_____
_____

## About you...

Name (*Mr/Mrs/Ms*) _____

Address _____

_____

_____ Postcode _____

Daytime tel nos _____

Email _____

Please only give us your mobile phone number or email if you wish to hear from us about other products and services from the AA and partners by text or mms, or email.

Which age group are you in?
Under 25 ☐   25–34 ☐   35–44 ☐   45–54 ☐   55–64 ☐   65+ ☐

How many trips do you make a year?
Less than one ☐   One ☐   Two ☐   Three or more ☐

Are you an AA member? Yes ☐   No ☐

## About your trip...

When did you book? m m / y y        When did you travel? m m / y y

How long did you stay? _____

Was it for business or leisure? _____

Did you buy any other travel guides for your trip? _____

If yes, which ones? _____
_____
_____

Thank you for taking the time to complete this questionnaire. Please send it to us as soon as possible, and remember, you do not need a stamp (*unless posted outside the UK*).

**AA** Travel Insurance call 0800 072 4168 or visit www.theAA.com